RYAN GiGGS SOCCER SKILLS

Ryan Giggs' Soccer Skills

with Sir Bobby Charlton

and Colin Cameron

BOXTREE

in association with
GRANADA TELEVISION
CHANNEL FOUR TELEVISION CORPORATION

Colin Cameron, who wrote this book with Ryan Giggs and Sir Bobby Charlton, is a specialist freelance sports writer. He graduated from Christ's College, Cambridge, in 1986 with a degree in Political Economy and joined Haymarket Publishing a year later, working there for four years and rising to deputy editor on the racing industry publication, Pacemaker Update. Since leaving Haymarket he has contributed to a wide cross-section of newspapers and magazines on sport and related issues and written a book, *The Contenders*, on athletics. He lives in London and wishes he could always get to Manchester for 3 o'clock on Saturdays to watch Ryan Giggs.

This book accompanies the television series 'Ryan Giggs' Soccer Skills' produced by Chrysalis Sport for Granada Television and Channel Four.

Ryan Giggs and Sir Bobby Charlton wish to thank Soccerpal® for their help in making the series.

First published in Great Britain in 1994 by Boxtree Limited

Text © Boxtree Limited 1994
Illustrations © Kurt Hoyte 1994

1 3 5 7 9 10 8 6 4 2

Designed by Martin Lovelock

Printed and bound in Glasgow by Bath Press Colour Books for

Boxtree Limited
Broadwall House · 21 Broadwall · London SE1 9PL

A CIP catalogue entry for this book is available from the British Library.

ISBN 1 85283 956 2

PHOTOGRAPH ACKNOWLEDGEMENTS
Front cover reproduced courtesy of Colorsport; back cover reproduced courtesy of Allsport.
pages: 1, 6, 11, 13, 22, 23, 24(left & right), 25, 29, 31, 34, 35, 37, 40(series), 44, 45, 58,
59, 62, 63, 67, 69, 73, 76, 79, 82, 88, 89, 95, 96 by Alan Sheldon, Matthew Ward,
Simon Wilkinson, reproduced courtesy of Chrysalis Sport;
pages: 2, 9, 50 by Alan Sheldon, reproduced courtesy of Vision Video Ltd;
pages: 8(left), 12(above), 17(below), 21, 27, 28, 30, 38, 42, 48, 54, 55, 57, 64, 71(above),
75, 80, 86, 87(above & below), 93, 94 reproduced courtesy of Empics;
pages: 8(right), 12(below), 17(above), 43, 47, 53, 60, 61(above & below), 74, 84
reproduced courtesy of Allsport;
pages: 16, 71(below), 72 reproduced courtesy of Colorsport;
page: 51(left) reproduced courtesy of the Kobal Collection;
page: 51(right) reproduced courtesy of Sportsline Photographic.

Contents

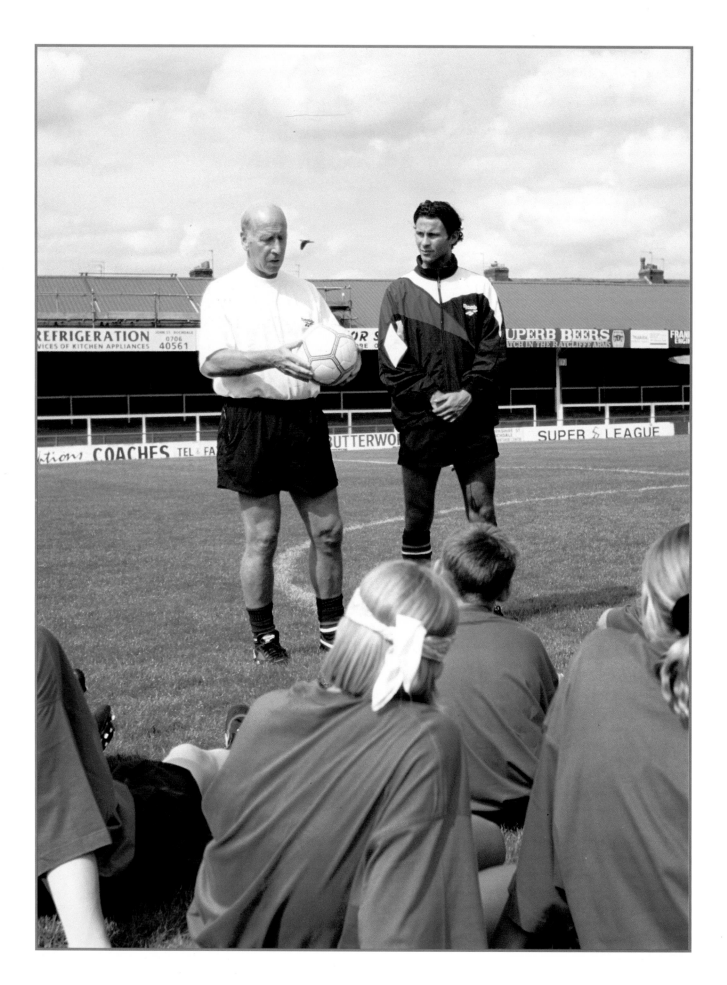

Introduction

Hi there,

If you're reading this, you'll be serious about soccer skills. For many people, football's a serious business. You're right to take pride in your performance, to want to get better, to improve your first touch, your dribbling, your corners and free kicks. It's right to want to play to the best of your ability. It means you'll get the most out of the game.

Always remember, though, that football is fun. Practice is, too. You'll enjoy it as well as the end product on the pitch. Football's a game that brings joy to millions of people all over the world. Football should always make you smile, even when you've lost. Even when it's a serious business.

We've certainly had fun working on the television series and video that go with this book. Putting together what you're going to read was great fun, too. And that's the way it should be. Football: the best game in the world. Always fun.

We both hope this book helps you with your game. The sketches recreate real match situations and put you in the thick of the action. Either you're on the attack watching it unfold, or you've got a great view of players using skill to beat defenders and score goals.

The photographs should help too. And when you've finished reading, always remember to enjoy it, from the kick around with your pals to eleven-a-side with your school or club.

Good luck with improving your skills

RYAN GIGGS

SIR BOBBY CHARLTON

Ryan Giggs

Ryan Giggs is Britain's most exciting young footballer. He plays for Manchester United, Britain's most exciting team, at Old Trafford, one of the best stadiums in the country. He made his international debut for Wales as a substitute in 1991, aged 17. On his first full appearance two years later he scored in a crucial World Cup qualifier.

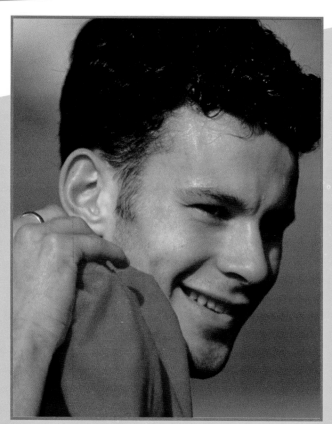

The hair style has changed, but the smile remains the same. There is plenty to smile about, too. Ryan Giggs already has a winner's medal collection that is the envy of many experienced fellow professionals.

It's a short career to date, but one already brimming with memories. So far, Giggs has picked up two Premier League winner's medals and played in successful League and FA Cup teams, a domestic clean sweep. If he avoids injury, he is set to enjoy another 15 years of top-class football and honours.

Ryan Giggs has pace and skill. It's what makes him such a thrilling sight. It prompted one commentator to say he was like a 'Porsche against a Mini' when leaving one Premier League full back in his slipstream. BMW would have been a more appropriate comparison – he drives one!

Born on 29 November 1973, Giggs remembers first playing football just before turning ten. 'I lived in Cardiff until I was seven and then we moved to Manchester. I think I started watching football around 1982. I remember the World Cup finals that year.'

Then it was on to Deans Youth Club, Salford Boys

and Manchester City before United's manager, Alex Ferguson entered the fray and personally signed Giggs as an apprentice aged 14. 'He came round to our house. He just knocked on the door. I'd supported United as a boy and always watched them, so you can imagine the excitement.'

Giggs began in the 'B' team before graduating to the 'A' team. After leaving school he quickly became a regular in the reserves and made a first appearance in the senior side, coming on as a substitute against Everton. Three years after Ferguson's first visit, there was a full home debut at Old Trafford, appropriately in the Manchester derby and the beginnings of a career that has already thrilled many at the Theatre of Dreams and beyond. George Best says he's 'a real superstar'. Many compare him to the former United star.

Off the field, Giggs is now much sought after for promotional work. His picture features on the front of countless magazines. There's been a video, articles, television appearances, and commentary work at the World Cup finals. Giggs remembers when he was at Deans, there seemed to be quite a few players better than him. 'At the time I didn't think I was that good.' Time spent at the FA School of Excellence once a week allowed Giggs to make strides on his contemporaries.

Since then, there's been more hard work, particularly on his skills, helped by the likes of Brian Kidd, assistant to Ferguson. Time practising his technique has helped him become the player he is today. Practice and hard work pays off when it comes to soccer skills.

Shooting at Goal

Shots at goal are what makes football such a brilliant game. They're the most exciting part of it – they mean goals. That's what the whole game is all about. Bobby Charlton had one of the most feared shots in the world. He's still England's all-time record goal scorer with 49 on target. Today, everyone in Britain knows about Ryan Giggs' shot and very soon they'll know about it in the rest of Europe – and even further afield with Wales – too. You'll get no better advice on hitting the target than from this pair. Giggs and Charlton have well-earned reputations for shots on goal. And, after all, shooting is what every player most wants to know about.

With two defenders after you, there's not much time so sticking to the key principles for shooting at goal is all the more important; keep your head steady and strike through the centre. Here the keeper is well positioned so you'd have to beat him with power as well as accuracy. And you'd have to be quick about it, too.

Ryan Giggs

'I'm no different to you, I love to score goals. I've mostly played up-front — either at centre forward or on the left wing where I usually start for United — so it's one of my jobs, but though it's work, I still love it! Scoring at Old Trafford or for Wales, there's no feeling like it.

At United we all love to practise shooting. After fitness work, Peter Schmeichel goes in goal for us. It's just like it is in the park, there are nine or ten of us all wanting to shoot. But we have to hold back a bit.

We don't all have a go at the same time like your warm up for an important Sunday morning game. Peter's a big man. It's not a good idea to hit him from six yards. You wouldn't want to get on the wrong side of him!

But, seriously, it's more organized than that. Shooting is too important to treat as a joke. No shots means no goals — apart from a few Mark Hughes headers! — so you've got to spend time improving your skill at one of the most important disciplines there is to learn.

Bobby used to score some great goals from miles out. He had a great shot. When you shoot you must keep your head over the ball like he did, otherwise it's out of the ground. It'll help you get more power, too, as well as keeping it in the stadium!

It's important to follow through too, even when

Following through, as Ryan does here, is very important in getting power into a shot at goal. It's also helpful as your strike will carry you towards goal, so you'll be well placed to snap up any rebounds if the keeper or a defender blocks. Then, if you finally find the target, it's celebrations.

Practise, practise, practise...

Shooting at goal is a crucial skill – after all, goals win matches – and the only way you'll improve is by spending time perfecting your technique on the training ground, against a wall or with a pal in the park. This goes for all your skills. Practice makes perfect. Great goal scorers like Ryan Giggs spend time working on their shooting. If he needs to then so do you. You'll never recreate exact goal mouth situations – even practice matches are a poor substitute for the real thing – but by practising , you'll be as ready as you can be for the moment when a chance falls to you during a game. Then, like Ryan here, it's head steady, keep it low, strike it clean and hit the target.

the shot is from close range. Again, this will help you generate power but it's also important because you'll be there for any rebounds if the keeper manages to block it. But don't try and hit the cover off the ball. Firstly, it's not the key to power – timing is. And secondly, you'll lose control and be even less likely to hit the target. And that's not much use. In fact, if you spot that the keeper's badly positioned it can be worth sacrificing some power for accuracy. You can use a side foot shot here to place the ball and take advantage of the keeper's misjudgment. If the keeper's left a gap, the important thing is to find it. Power is less important.

It's a real advantage to be able to shoot with both feet. Everyone favours one side – I much prefer the ball on my left foot – but ability to shoot with either is a real skill. It adds an extra dimension to your game.

This is where practice is really important. As an apprentice, I was getting into scoring positions and wasting them, so I spent time in the gym striking a ball against a wall with my right foot to improve it. Hopefully, it's getting better now. You can improve your 'wrong' foot by doing the same, against a wall or with a pal. Once you're confident you can have a go with it in a match.

Training and five-a-sides are when you can perfect your technique for that first strike in a game. It's no good strolling around in five-a-side. It won't make you any better. Play as close to match speed as you can without risking injury. It's much better preparation. What defenders never allow you in a game is time. Chances to shoot are precious; you don't want to waste them because you can't go the pace. Scoring's the best feeling in the world. All the hard work is definitely worth the effort.'

Bobby Charlton
'Ryan's too kind! He's right, though. I did score some long-rangers, for both England and United. The more I practised the further back I went until I was completely confident. I worked on my timing on the training ground so that in a match I could take a pop from quite a bit outside the box.

You've got to put the effort in, though. When it comes to shooting, it's much easier to be a defender than an attacker. It's great when the ball screams into the net, but when you're trying to get a shot in, you're under pressure. And the odds favour the defence.

Think about it. There are defenders, and a goalkeeper who can handle the ball, all trying to stop you squeezing it into an eight yards by eight foot space. Defenders have the whole world to aim for. You have to hit the target while they can kick it anywhere. It's not surprising, really, that it sometimes ends 0–0. The odds are against the attacker.

That said, the most important thing to remember when it comes to shots on goal is: DON'T BE AFRAID TO MISS. Sometimes you've got a half chance and a team mate is screaming for a pass. Don't worry, have a go. All the great players have missed a hat-full of chances in the process of scoring heavily. No one expects you to be any different and you never know if a pass to your pal will produce a better opportunity. Go on, have a shot. When you attack, the move should always end with a shot on goal.

Don't worry about how it looks. You may get only a half chance in the whole game and the ball may never sit up for that perfect strike in your head. Great strikers knock the ball in with their toes if they can't get anything else on the ball. Romario showed this in the World Cup. In the semi-final against Sweden he had time to measure his finish, when the cross came over, and head it cleanly into the net, but his first goal of the tournament was a completely different strike. He was tightly marked by the Russian defence and all he had time for was a little nudge with the outside of his boot. But he made good contact; he got his shot in. From close range, it was impossible to defend against. One–nil to Brazil and off to the World Cup Final.

You won't get much time when the chance comes. Romario had a split second. You have to assess where the keeper and defenders are in the time available. Above all, take the chance at the first opportunity and strike the ball as cleanly as you can in the general direction of the goal. If your shot isn't set for goal a deflection might turn it in. The keeper has little chance if the path of your shot changes. Give it a chance to happen.

As a youngster I was always told to strike a shot as hard and as cleanly as I could and not worry about exactly where it was going. If you don't know where it's heading, the keeper's sure not to know either! Some of the dads will remember Bert Trautmann

It's easy to see from this situation why the odds usually favour the defence when you're trying to get a shot on goal. The two defenders only have to get a foot in here to block, and the keeper is well placed to save either the low hard shot or one that's placed. But don't be afraid to miss and don't worry about how it will look if the ball ends up in the stands. This sort of chance can end up among the spectators, but you should still shoot from the position. Every move should end with a shot on goal, even when you're under pressure.

who played for Manchester City. Give Bert an idea where your shot was going and he would save it every time. If you look up and pick a spot, the chances are the keeper will also have been let in on your little secret about where it's going.

Outside the box, you may have a little more time. There will be other options, too, and plenty of noise from team mates pointing them out to you. But if you have the shot, don't be afraid to use it. Strike it sweetly and on target and your colleagues won't have much to complain about. You've got to take the chance to score if it falls to you and you've got the skill to exploit it.

Ryan's already mentioned how important it is to keep the ball down. You must strike through the top half of the ball to keep it under the crossbar. Make as good a contact as you can. Timing is everything, particularly outside the box when the keeper has more time to make a save. As I mention when we talk later about free kicks, nowadays the ball is much lighter and softer than in my playing days, so there's no need to try and hit the cover off it. It won't give you extra power. Timing will.

It will come with practice. Practice helps shooting become instinctive. The more you practise, the further back you'll be able to go. That's what happened for me. There's no reason why it can't happen for you.

Even the best players have to practise. It has always been the way at Manchester United, from the days when I played right through to today's generation, Ryan's team mates. Shooting will round off a fitness session to give the players some ball work: to tune them up for a game on Saturday or Wednesday, just some finishing touches on the main work; half chances, shots outside the box, free kicks, shots from corners and crosses. Everyone works on them, even the stars. Shooting is no different to any football skill.

Your hard work will pay off on the pitch with improved performances. It's always the way with football.'

Rituals and Superstitions

Football players are a funny lot. Some salute magpies, others wear the same suit every Saturday and always put the left boot on before the right. Team mates sometimes argue over who is going to be the last person out of the dressing room. The dressing room is a hotbed of rituals and superstitions. If a player thinks he'll have a good game if he puts his shorts on before his socks, then it's a brave colleague who tries to persuade him otherwise.

Ryan isn't very superstitious. He doesn't have a pre-match ritual. He makes his own luck on the field. 'I don't really bother with all that. Sometimes, if I've had a good game the week before, I'll try and do exactly the same things the morning before the next match, but that's about it really. I don't have a special suit or anything like that. To be honest, I don't think it really matters.'

But don't be fooled. Ryan has his wary moments all right! Even though he is safer doing it than crossing the road, Ryan worries about flying. In fact, he hates it. But it's only when he is a passenger that he frets. When he's the pilot, it's no problem. In America flying between venues at the World Cup, he was allowed to take the controls at 30,000ft for a few minutes. 'It was pretty straightforward, no looping the loop. I don't like flying, but it was definitely better when I was at the controls.'

Paul Ince, Ryan's favourite on and off-pitch mate, is more neurotic. 'Incey always puts his shirt on as he's going down the tunnel and comes out last.'

Unless he's captain, that is!

At ground level on the pitch, Incey and Ryan have their own superstitious celebratory ritual, a thank you to Lady Luck after they've scored.

Well done Ryan! Another goal for Manchester United and team mate Roy Keane is first on the scene to offer congratulations to the scorer.

Paul Ince and Ryan have a celebration ready if either scores. Their routine is pretty conventional, though, compared with some at the World Cup.

goal samba. A Nigerian, Fenidi George, went as far as impersonating a dog, going down on all fours and even answering an imaginary call of nature, after scoring for the African champions. A team mate, Rashidi Yekini, satisfied himself with hanging from the net and chanting his father's name into the television camera, a personal thank you for his country's first goal at the game's highest level.

'Some of the Manchester United players have their own thing – Lee Sharpe has his own dance – and a lot of players at other clubs are starting to do something like it. Maybe they've been watching too much American football.

'I think I'm finished with celebrations now, I'll leave it at the normal one with Incey. No Nigerian celebrations from me!' Perhaps it's for the best. After all, in Italy players have been known to find themselves stripped nearly naked by over-enthusiastic fans. And in the Premier League now there is also the chance you'll get booked for time-wasting if you over-do the fun and games. That said, it didn't stop Jurgen Klinsmann celebrating a first goal for his new club, Tottenham Hotspur, against Sheffield Wednesday with a full-length dive

onto the Hillsborough turf. The fans loved it – even Wednesday supporters had to laugh – and the German's new team mates joined in the fun making it football's first synchronized swimming exhibition. Maybe it's the start of a new trend.

'We have our own little celebration we worked out at training one day. After the ball's in the net it's "gimme five, draw your pistols and then shuffle back sharp shooting with fingers cocked and firing".'

The fans have their own special accompaniment. To the tune of 'Robin Hood, Robin Hood', its 'Ryan Giggs, Ryan Giggs, running down the wing, Ryan Giggs, Ryan Giggs, running down the wing, feared by the blues, loved by the reds, Ryan Giggs, Ryan Giggs, Ryan Giggs'.

Ryan and Incey's routine is pretty conventional compared with some of the more outlandish celebrations. Other players have their own personal styles which take a bit of explaining. The World Cup in America was the scene of many a bizarre post-

Free Kicks

Blackburn Rovers and Belgium know that Ryan Giggs takes a great free kick. Blackburn know because he scored his favourite Manchester United goal against them to mark a first league title for 26 years. Belgium were on the receiving end against Wales on his full debut. Both were long-range shots perfect for the occasion.

Ryan Giggs

'Who do you think's got the hardest shot at United? Denis Irwin? Eric Cantona? Me?! It's actually Andrei Kanchelskis. But there's more to free kicks than power. Accuracy is at least as important. And sometimes it's invention that's the key. You don't always have a direct shot at goal. Sometimes you've got to look to do something else to break down a defence.

What is always true is that, when you get a free kick near the penalty box, you must finish with a shot on goal. It can be a straight shot or a pass for someone else to shoot. BUT GET THAT SHOT IN.

Roberto Baggio is a great free kick expert. I enjoy the Italian football on Channel 4 on Sunday because you see players like Baggio in dead ball situations where they have a chance to show real flair. Zola is another great free kick specialist. He seems to score from at least two out of three free kicks.

Baggio and Zola are masters of the direct shot. In the World Cup there was a great example of the other type of free kick the pass to shoot. Sweden's goal against Romania – scored by Brolin, a team mate of Zola's at Parma – was the result of a great ball while the defensive wall was bracing itself for a direct shot. Mixing it up like that can cause confusion. And as long as it ends up with a strike on goal and is not too elaborate, why not try something different? It keeps the defence guessing.

I take my fair share of free kicks in the danger zone which is very handy in keeping my seasonal tally of goals up. I'd hope to be on the mark five or six times a season. But that doesn't mean I am always clamouring to take them. Usually, if it's on the right I'll have a go. Being left footed, I can curl one in over the wall. But if it's on the left, Denis will have a go. The centre is Eric's speciality. And don't forget Andrei's power.

The great thing is that we're all capable of scoring. If one of us really

When you're faced with a wall like the one here, a free kick has to have height as well as power. The wall blocks the direct shot to the far post and the keeper has covered the near post. Your team mate on the end of the wall can make space for a shot by peeling off the end as you run up. The hole in the wall looks big enough for the ball, but you'd have to be very confident about your accuracy to risk a shot through it.

fancies it then the others will let him have a go. We don't argue about it. It sorts itself out.

You know the moment that you've hit it whether it's on target. But sometimes it hits the bar or the keeper makes a great save. That's very disappointing. The wall sometimes obscures your view and you might think it's in, and then the keeper comes across in time because you haven't hit it hard enough. That's the most disappointing moment. You've got it over the wall so you've achieved your first objective, and it's on target. Then it's like the goal is snatched away from you!

They couldn't do that with my goal against Blackburn. It has to be the most memorable of my career so far at United. It was the occasion and the feeling after scoring it more than the goal itself.

United hadn't won the championship in 26 years. After blowing it the year before, it was great finally to end the spell and the game was all set up to be a huge party for us. We'd already clinched the title and were going to be receiving the trophy on the night so the game had the makings of a great finale. All that was needed was a win. Blackburn were desperate to ruin our party celebrations and I was so pleased when it went in and cancelled out their opening strike. I didn't think it would get near the goal post, let alone go in the net. I went wild. Then Paul Ince and Gary Pallister added to it and we ran out comfortable 3–1 winners.

I caught that one perfectly. Good contact is obviously essential. It's crucial that you watch the ball for this. If you want to hit it straight you should make contact with the bone in the top of your foot for maximum power. Strike through the centre of the ball.

Power isn't everything, though. The free kick has got to be accurate. It is always worth sacrificing a bit of power if it means you'll definitely get it on target. The funny thing is, if you try and hit the cover off the ball, you'll get less power than if you steady yourself and concentrate on timing the shot. Power comes through timing and that means everything working together. If you try and force it, you'll lose it.

If you want to bend it, hit the opposite side of the ball to the direction that you're trying to swerve it. You can swerve it quite well using your instep but you might lose a bit of power. Only use the instep if the added accuracy means the keeper won't get to it.

To get some extra swerve it's sometimes worth varying your run up, coming at the ball at an angle. Look at the Brazilians. They are brilliant at it.

If there's a wall you'll need height. You'll have to lean back for this and strike the ball just below centre. But be careful. The ball can easily end up in the stands. And make sure you follow through. You've seen the pictures in the paper of the player in the air after having taken a pop. Make sure you finish like they do. Hopefully, the keeper will be picking the ball out of the net shortly afterwards.'

The keeper has arranged the wall well for the free kick. You'd have to get height on your shot as a low hard strike will simply be blocked. The striker here has approached the ball at an angle which helps generate swerve. This makes it much harder for the keeper if you place the ball in the far corner. It is always going away from him. Although the wall is an obstacle to a direct shot, the keeper's view shows how it can be an advantage to you. Here it obscures the ball. This means the keeper sees it late and has less time to react.

Bobby Charlton

'The World Cup saw some great free kicks. Stoichkov scored with a direct shot by bending the ball over the wall. It helped Bulgaria knock the Germans out of the competition. Their goalkeeper had to commit himself to one side and once the ball had cleared the wall it was impossible for him to get over and cover. A direct shot is the norm these days. The ball is lighter and softer than in my day; it's easier to bend. But Sweden and Brolin showed us that the direct shot is not always the most effective way of scoring.

The free kick has to be reasonably in line with the goal for you to opt for the direct shot. Directly in front of goal is about as dangerous a situation as you're going to get. There'll be a wall as it's too much of a risk to give someone with a tremendous shot a free strike, even from as far out as 25 yards.

But a good wall – even an angle – doesn't mean

Who'll it be?

Ryan is just one of the Manchester United team who has a reputation for scoring direct from a free kick. It means that wherever the free kick is around the box, there will be someone who can have a shot at goal. Denis Irwin (right) has a strong right foot that makes him ideal for free kicks outside the box to the left of the goal. His goal against Liverpool in the three-all draw at Anfield in the 1993/4 season was one of the strikes of the year.

you can't shoot. If you're good enough, have a go. Rivelino was great at hitting a very tight target area from an angle, wall or no wall. I remember in the Sixties John Charles scoring for Leeds when we had a substantial wall. He hit a thunderbolt and our keeper, Ray Wood, never saw it. Neither did the wall; we'd all turned our backs on it!

We should have been braver really, although he did hit it very hard! But, seriously, the wall must do its job. As I've said, professionals who specialize in taking free kicks are just too good to be allowed a clear sight of goal. You have to cut down the options and limit the target area as much as you can. Otherwise it's going to be a goal against.

In attack, the wall is just one of the considerations you have to weigh up. Wind is a factor too, when you're deciding what to do with a free kick A strong breeze might make you think twice about having a go. Best to look at other options if it's blowing a gale.

Sometimes you've just got to accept that the direct shot isn't on. Wind is one reason for opting to try something different to a direct strike. So is distance. If you are too far from goal a shot will be a waste of a good attacking position. Distance is less of a consideration in today's game. Today's lighter ball means you can have a go from much further out and get swerve and dip to carry you over the wall and under the bar. But, you've still got to be prepared sometimes to consider an alternative to a shot on goal.

Variety is important. The odd variation keeps the keeper guessing. If the keeper doesn't know what to expect, he's more likely to produce a mistake. The

The wall means Ryan has to lean back when he makes contact to get under the ball and give the free kick some height to clear it. Ryan follows through after the shot. As with all shots on goal, the follow through is very important as it gives you extra power.

Russian international Andrei Kanchelskis (above) has the hardest shot at Manchester United. Other continental players also have power which, combined with accuracy, is the key to free kick taking. Roberto Baggio, Gianfranco Zola and Hristo Stoichkov have all impressed in Europe with free kicks.

keeper might drop the ball for someone to score from the rebound if he's worried that you could be lining up to curl one, to chip or try something other than a direct shot. Try the shot if it's on, but make sure the keeper and the defenders can't be sure that's what you've planned.

Above all, keep composed. It's difficult. Everyone loves to see the ball crashing into the back of the net from 25 yards like a rocket, but you mustn't waste the chance. Don't be over enthusiastic; it's a

great opportunity. Steady yourself.

Time on the training ground will certainly pay dividends in the match. Even the great players weren't born with the ability just to step up to the ball and score. They've perfected the skill of striking the ball with swerve and power.

The technique is simple, as Ryan has explained. The power comes from addressing the ball from just behind it. If the wall is poorly placed and the keeper badly positioned you might be able to strike directly at goal, but if you need to clear the wall then get under the ball a little.

Giggs' against Blackburn was a great effort. What a goal. But don't forget the variations. A short pass can change the angle. Eric Cantona's strike against Arsenal at Old Trafford in 1993 was a perfect example of this. A little pass then bang. Brilliant. And great for the fans.'

Training

Nearly all professional footballers love the game, but many are considerably less enthusiastic about training. It's the least glamorous part of their work. Without it, though, the end product would suffer. Players have to be fit to perform, especially for the gruelling English domestic season, the toughest in the world.

Ryan trains with Manchester United at The Cliff. It's been the club's key preparatory venue for years. Ryan gets fit after a pre-season holiday on the same stretch that Bobby Charlton was put through his paces when he was a player. Brian Kidd, too, trained there when he was a United player before leaving the club only to return, years later, to take up a coaching post, eventually becoming assistant to Alex Ferguson.

Kiddo is as aware as anyone that training at the same ground day in, day out can get monotonous.

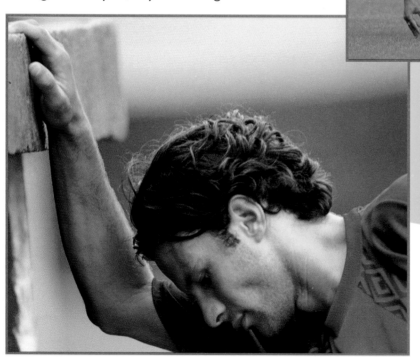

Ryan likes training. He looks forward to it. Pre-season training is hard, but once the league programme has started the routine is less gruelling. Then, stretching the legs, some running and a bit of five-a-side is all that's needed to stay fit.

'Brian Kidd's been to some of the continental clubs to see how they train and is always coming out with new ideas to keep it interesting. It's a serious business, but if you enjoy it you'll perform better.'

Pre-season training is hard, particularly for the older players who may lose fitness faster than youngsters like Ryan over the summer. Even he, a naturally fit athlete, feels tired at this time of the year.

'We do a lot more running in a day of pre-season training – 3,000 metres to start with and 6,000 metres to wind up the session. Most of the lads won't do anything over the summer so we do a lot of stamina work in the first week back, with some sprinting at the end. The long distance work is never competitive but sprints can get quite personal.

'The ball is introduced to us again quite early. Kiddo wants us on the ball as soon as possible to get us back into the swing of things.'

Once the team is into the league programme, the emphasis changes. 'We do less running because we

Even during training, there's always a chance for Ryan to snatch a chat with Paul Ince. Alex Ferguson suspects they are joined at the hip!

get fit from playing games. It's more five-a-side games, with some running and stretching.'

Ryan has just started to do some extra weights and circuit training to add a bit more power to his upper body. But he's already come a long way from his apprentice days, training all day. 'I used to train in the morning and do weights in the afternoon. There was also great emphasis on skill with little five-a-side games. Most forwards have a skill for taking free kicks or corners or crossing or shooting and mine was nurtured from an early age.'

The combination of skill and stamina training means there's little chance of Ryan flagging in the last 15 minutes, even in games at the end of a long, hard season.

Corner Taking

A corner really get the crowd going. It's deep in attacking territory, it's a chance for the big men to add their weight and height to the forward line, and it's a great opportunity to put the ball right into the heart of the danger zone, the penalty box, and force a goal.

Ryan Giggs

'I've only started to realize how important corners are since we won our second Premier League title. I used simply to hit them. Now I take more care. If you win a corner, you've got to make sure you get a good cross in. Sometimes the pressure is on, you're 1-0 down and there isn't much time left on the clock, but you've got to compose yourself and make sure you make good contact with the ball.

Denis Irwin usually takes the corners for United on the left and I have responsibility for the ones from the right. If either of us is not going well, the other will have a go from the other side, an outswinger

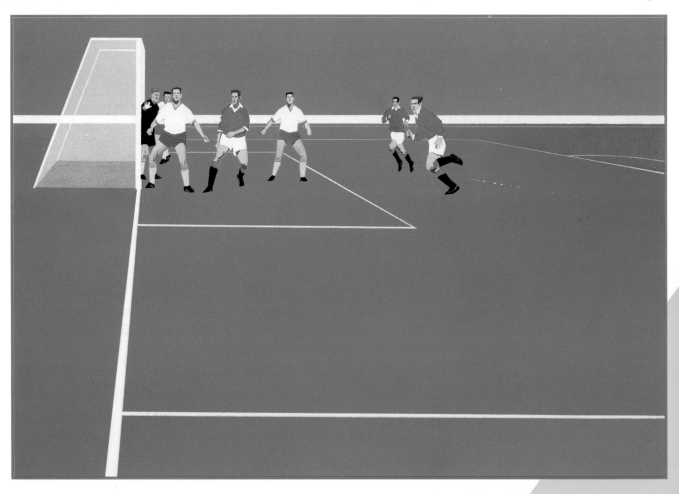

instead of the natural inswinger my left foot and his right foot produce from our normal sides.

I came up against a problem with this switch when an eagle-eyed linesman signalled that a corner I took from the left had crossed the goal line before starting to swing out with the spin. Lee Sharpe took over from me after that for the rest of the game. I'll keep an eye on that in the future when Denis and I swop sides as the variety of corners is important. We want to have the option of the switch. It all helps to keep defenders on their nerve ends. When they don't know what to expect, they are more likely to make mistakes.

When I take a corner, I'm closer to the crowd than at any time in the game (unless I'm on the bench!). You have to block that out and concentrate on the job in hand. This is really important when I'm playing away from home and the crowd are giving it some stick. At grounds like West Ham and Queens Park Rangers there are only three or four paces between the corner flag and the fans. I usually take four or five paces if there's space, but when it's a squeeze, I'll make do with a couple less. You

don't want to get too close to the opposition.

At Old Trafford, it's a bit more friendly and there's more space, but you've still got to concentrate and get in a good cross. Keep it away from the keeper and find a red shirt.

We practise corners after we've done the main training session with Alex Ferguson and Brian Kidd. I might stay on a bit with Incey and swing a few in for him. He attacks the near post and only needs a touch to score.

In matches, Steve Bruce and Gary Pallister, United's big men, come up for corners and I'll always look out for them so they can exploit their height.

You must be aware of your colleagues' movements in the penalty box when you are taking a corner to see who has lost their marker. Here, you have team mates available at the near post, centrally placed, and at the far post for a deep cross.

Paul Ince (right) usually attacks the near post at corners. If he gets on the end of an inswinger from Ryan then it's very difficult to defend against. He needs only a touch and the keeper has no time to react to the change of direction.

from a corner, they'll be the first to congratulate you, even though you're tucked away on the sidelines.'

Bobby Charlton

'Professional teams spend a lot of time working on corners. They'd work out on the training ground who runs to the near post, who runs to the far post, who is static and who makes the decoy run to give the big men some extra space. It's difficult to pin-point any cross, even a corner when it's a dead ball situation. Not many goals come from direct headers – even for United! The main thing is to create problems for the defence, a bit of uncertainty in the minds of the centre halves and the keeper by getting the ball into the danger zone.

Manchester United scored six of their 80 league goals in the 1993/4 season from corners. Ryan's international colleague Mark Hughes (left) is always dangerous from such set plays. The central defensive partnership of Steve Bruce and Gary Pallister turns into an attacking force for corners as they usually come up for them. Their height makes them dangerous.

When United force a corner on the right, it's perfect for Ryan's inswinger (right). Having created the chance, it's then up to him to make good contact. In this situation, it's important your basic technique is right; watch the ball, strike through the centre and follow through for the power you'll need to reach your team mates in the box. Corners are great opportunities. Don't waste them through having poor technique.

You've got to vary corners. It makes them much harder to defend against if the defence is unsure where the cross is going. Low and hard or deep and floated, inswingers, outswingers, they can all be effective. The short corner is an option, too, if a team mate is quick-thinking enough. It takes a defender out of the box and gives the attacker a little bit more space. The angle of attack is different, too. It all goes towards the whole point of a corner - to unsettle the defence with a cross that is difficult to defend against. But if it's a simple cross into the box that's the option then it's back to basics again: good contact, a clean strike and some height and pace. Achieve these and the rest is up to your team mates. And if they score

If your big men have stayed back because of the state of the match, or your forwards don't measure up against their marker, the inswinger – Ryan's speciality – is very effective. A corner swung in to the near post and flicked on is very difficult to defend against, even when there are plenty of players covering back and man-to-man marking your best headers.

Ryan's point about short corners is a good one. They're an option when your full back or a midfielder is unmarked. If the pass is on to the corner of the penalty box, there is a chance of a shot or a cross from a different angle that the defence isn't expecting. It's something you can work on. The extra time gives smaller players a few more seconds to lose their taller markers. Keep an eye open for it.

Technically, taking a corner is no different to striking a pass or a free kick. An inswinger or out swinger is just bending the ball. Strike the outside and set it spinning. When you practise passing and improving your accuracy, you'll be improving your corners, too. You can do it against a wall or with a pal standing away from you the same distance between the corner flag and the goal. Youngsters sometimes struggle to get the ball into the box from the corner. Don't worry if you're not strong enough yet. You will be soon. Until then, you can work variations on short corners. A ball along the goal line for a pal to run on to is a good way of cutting down the distance you have to cover with your cross. Mind it doesn't go out of play, though. A corner is a great opportunity. Your team has worked hard to get the ball upfield. They'll be annoyed if you waste their efforts. Make sure you get the ball into the box. Cause some chaos.'

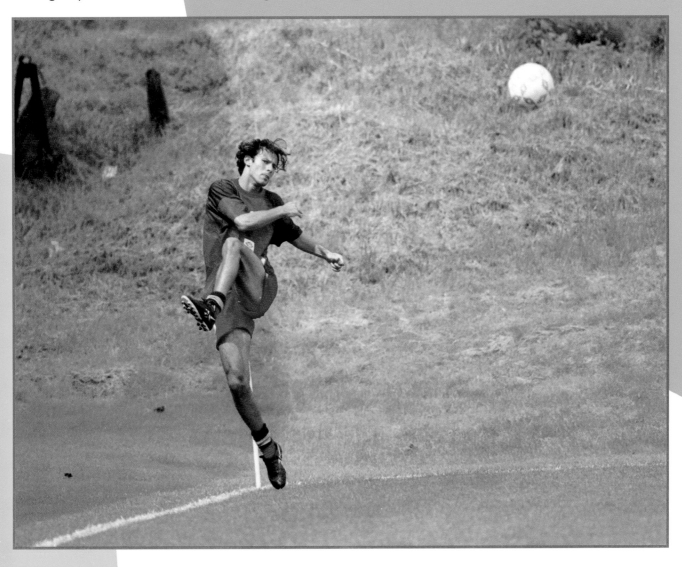

Penalty Taking

Penalties are more important today than they've ever been. Any player, even the goalkeeper, can be called upon to take a penalty in a sudden death shootout. Ryan and Bobby have different views on spot kicks but both agree, YOU'VE GOT TO SCORE.

Ryan Giggs

'I don't take penalties for United, that's Eric Cantona's job, but I have taken them throughout my career. I took them when I played for England Schoolboys and for my district side in Manchester. I scored an important one for England at Wembley when we were playing Belgium Schoolboys and the game was really evenly balanced. It wasn't a great penalty but the keeper went the wrong way.

I missed a crucial one at Old Trafford a few seasons ago in an FA Cup game. It was a replay against Southampton which went to a shootout after extra time. I thought the keeper was going to move so I blasted it straight down the middle. He didn't! Out we went.

I'd have no problems with taking one again. It's all about confidence. You can tell if a player is going to miss from the way they place the ball and run up to strike it. Anyone can miss if they have any doubts about finding the net. If you are confident, there is every chance you'll convert.

Mr Confidence

If Manchester United are awarded a penalty, then Mr Confidence, Eric Cantona, steps up for the task. Cantona has scored three penalties in his last two visits to Wembley; two in the FA Cup Final against Chelsea and one in the Charity Shield against Premier League runners-up Blackburn. The Frenchman usually aims to place the ball to the side of the keeper. Neither Dmitri Kharine in goal for Chelsea in the Cup Final or Tim Flowers, Blackburn's keeper, guessed which way he was going to shoot. On both occasions, few in the stadium expected Cantona to miss. He did not disappoint. He's so confident from the spot and is always calm, even in front of a Wembley full house.

The 1994 Cup Final showed this. We got two penalties against Chelsea in our 4–0 win, and they were no problem. Eric Cantona was the most confident man on the pitch, even in the stadium! If you needed someone to take a penalty in front of 80,000 fans, with millions watching on television, Eric was your man. Not because he was the best striker of the ball, or the best placer – although he might well be – but because he just knew he was going to score. He did it again in the Charity Shield, when we beat Blackburn 2–0.

Apparently, Steve Bruce didn't watch the Cup Final penalties. He watched the crowd. He knew soon enough that we'd scored. What a roar! I have to watch because I am following in from the edge of the box. Brucey's far away (although he used to be our spot kick man before Eric) and doesn't have to worry about rebounds.

When you're taking a penalty yourself, BE POSITIVE AND DON'T CHANGE YOUR MIND. It

Changing your strategy for a penalty after you've started your run up usually ends as a disaster. Ryan has missed penalties before through indecision. Here, as he steps up to take a penalty, he has already decided on a plan and will stick to it. Indecision, not the keeper, is his greatest enemy. It doesn't matter if you prefer to use power or placement and accuracy when you're taking a penalty, stick to the plan and expect to convert it. Then it becomes a very straightforward affair.

doesn't matter how you score, there are plenty of different ways to hit the target, but decide on one and stick to it. You can chip it – Socrates, the great Brazilian from the 1980s did that – blast it, side foot it, dummy one way, or just strike it as you would a pass, but stick to your original plan.

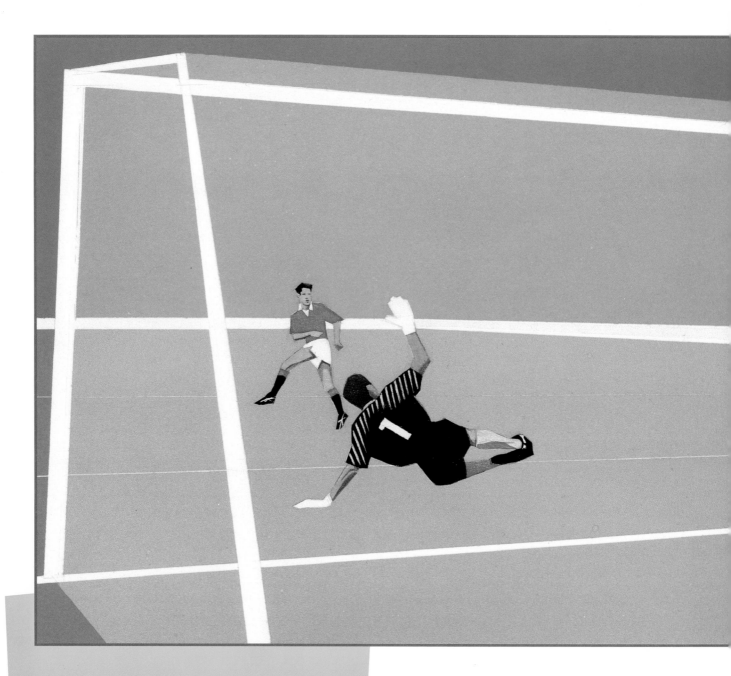

This penalty is unstoppable. The keeper has either decided which way to go and guessed wrong or has been fooled by the penalty taker's run up and gone the wrong way. The keeper looks as though he has moved before the penalty was struck, and the referee is close on hand to insist that it's retaken if it's saved, but he's not needed here. The set up also shows how much the penalty situation favours the attacker. The keeper has to protect a large area and the striker is only 12 yards from goal. Even if the keeper had gone the right way here, it's doubtful he would have got anywhere near the ball.

Andrei Kanchelskis toe punts them, but he never changes his mind in the middle of his run-up, even if his style is slightly unorthodox, so he usually scores.

After the Southampton miss, I'd probably place them now, but it really doesn't matter what your method is. I can't repeat it often enough, BE CONFIDENT. When I have taken and missed penalties it's because I've been thinking about missing them. And when you do that, it's exactly what happens.'

Bobby Charlton 'I once missed two
penalties in one match: England versus Scotland in

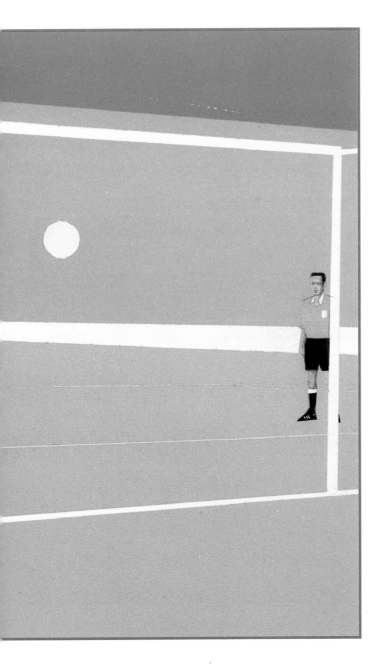

corner are taking a terrible risk. If it goes over the top it's such a waste.

Ryan's right, being confident is the most important thing, and being comfortable with your method. But for me after the Scotland game, I decided the best way was to hit the ball hard. The ones I missed were when I tried to side foot it and the keeper guessed right and saved.

If you pick the right spot and strike it cleanly, the keeper is very lucky to save it. Some players watch to see which way the keeper is going to go, but to me that is indecision. You are unsure in your own mind where it is going to go as you run up to the ball and that's an added complication you don't really need. Hit it well and it doesn't matter which way the keeper goes.

Power was my way. If you decide to side foot it, like Eric Cantona, then that's fine, but I can't really recommend it. We're not all as good as Eric! And the real blaster can't miss as long as it's on target and it's not straight at the keeper.

When you are deciding whether to blast or place, one thing worth bearing in mind is how many times a penalty is retaken today. It's not very often, is it? You have to rely on the referee making sure the keeper does not move before the ball is struck, as most keepers try to do. They steal a split second which can sometimes be the difference between a save and a goal. Maybe power is the most effective way to counter this modern trend.

The most important thing, though, is how you feel in yourself. You go back to basics, head over the ball, address it correctly, strike through it using the right part of your foot, follow through in case the keeper saves it. It's everything you are told as a young player by your coach at the beginning of your career.

Everyone should practise. Shootouts are part of the game now. The World Cup was decided by one. I have missed plenty and, as Ryan remembers, so has he. But he was unlucky. He'll make sure the next one's away from the keeper. He'll score, and so will you if you stick to basics and be confident.'

front of 134,000 at Hampden. Ugh! The first time wasn't my fault. I shot and the keeper could only get a hand to it before it crept over the line, but a team mate had encroached into the box so I had to retake it. Second time, I missed altogether.

But, bad memories aside, a penalty is a great chance to score. You get to place the ball, you can use either foot, no one can tackle you, and the goal is only 12 yards away.

Most of all, people want to see the ball in the back of the net. If it's a big game and one of your players tries to be flash and it's saved...oh dear. Not good. The players who try and put it in the top

Preparation

Ryan Giggs spends more time preparing than he does playing for Manchester United. Never mind the training, the pre-match preparatory routine lasts longer than the game itself – even when there's extra time. Preparation is everything.

It begins, hopefully, with some good sleep the night before a game and ends with a walk down the tunnel. Then it's fingers crossed.

'I usually sleep well the night before. I don't suffer from nerves really. If it's an afternoon home game at Old Trafford, we don't have to be at the ground until midday – I usually get there at about 12.20 and get shouted at – so I can have a lie-in. Evening kick-offs mean we get a sleep in the afternoon. Away games sometimes mean a hotel the night before. It can be boring staying away from home for the night. You get there by 7pm, eat and then go to your room to relax. I share with Paul Ince, I always have done. On the whole I prefer home games.'

Close to a game, Ryan has to watch what he eats. He needs plenty of energy, plenty of carbohydrates (beefburgers!) to draw on during the 90 minutes. On match day itself, it's crucial he has the right food before the game.

'We have a pre-match meal arranged for us at Old Trafford by a dietician who watches what we eat. I usually have something light, chicken or pasta. You can have anything as long as it's light: fish, potatoes. Nothing heavy on your stomach.'

The dressing room is where preparation becomes more personal and tense. It's less than 90 minutes to kick-off when Ryan links up with his team mates there.

Late again! Ryan often has to rush to meet the deadlines manager Alex Ferguson sets for arrival at the training ground and Old Trafford.

'Not many of us suffer from nerves, we just have a bit of a joke. The television is on in the dressing room. I quite like watching a bit. Others read the programme. The mobile phones go off about an hour before kick-off, except Paul Parker's, he's always on his.'

An hour before the game, they are joined by the 'gaffer', Alex Ferguson, for a team talk. Once the manager's finished, the players are left to their own individual routines and go out for a warm-up on the pitch. It's a chance for the fans to say hello to their favourites and an opportunity for the players to get the legs moving. 'It's nothing too strenuous, just a stretch.' Then it's back to the dressing room for a bit before the game itself.

It's slightly different for Wales. 'We have a chat in the morning before the game and then the time at the ground is our own.'

But for both United and Wales, the importance of preparation in the crucial hours before a game is not to be underestimated.

Rounding the Keeper

An open net is the best sight in football. No defenders, no goalkeeper. You can't miss. (At least, you shouldn't!) The last line of defence is sometimes the toughest customer stopping you getting there. They can use their hands, they're sometimes the biggest player on the pitch, they have only to put you off your stride and they've done their job. Ryan Giggs is outstanding at making sure they don't. Rounding the keeper requires a lot of skill and some cool finishing. But it's worth it for that open goal.

A keeper who has spread himself well is a difficult proposition. His hands are poised to take the ball and his body has covered the goal making a direct shot a risky option. He has left unguarded the upper half of the net, but a flick over him is a tricky skill. Pace should take you round him as he is grounded and committed to robbing you. You'll probably have an open goal if you negotiate him successfully. The only difficulty then might be that he's forced you wide. You'll need a cool head to find the target from a narrow angle.

Ryan prefers to use his pace to go round the keeper, one on one, if he can. It's his greatest strength against the keeper, who is often less mobile. By using it he dictates to the keeper and deals with the situation on his own terms, improving his chances of scoring.

Ryan Giggs

'I scored a goal going round the keeper in a Coca Cola Cup semi-final against Sheffield Wednesday. The back pass fell a bit short and I nipped in and went round the keeper, Kevin Pressman, and slotted it in from a tight angle.

I knew it was going in as soon as I hit it – although it just missed the post before crossing the line. I peeled away straight after I'd shot to celebrate. It's a great feeling.

I beat Pressman with pace. For me that's the best way to go round a keeper as you've the advantage. When you're running straight at the goal, the keeper is not the quickest player on the field by a long way. If you try to trick your way to goal the keeper might not buy the dummies and there's still something blocking your path to goal. In a one-on-one situation, you can dictate, so use your pace.

Pace also means the defence has little time to recover. If you delay your move towards goal, the poor defender who's gifted you the chance to score may get back and tackle. Believe me, they'll be desperate to. And even if they're aren't personally to blame, the goal is under serious threat.

The keeper's job is to make the goal look as small

as possible. Peter Schmeichel is very good at doing that. He is so big and agile he makes the ball and goal look tiny. Some keepers try to intimidate you as well by throwing dummies – it's not just wingers who have tricks up their sleeves. But it doesn't matter who the keeper is, you've got to dictate. Take them on on your own terms. If you're right footed then try and get the ball on your favoured side. I try and get it on the left if I can.

It's a good idea to get into the box, too. It ups the stakes for the keeper – a foul and it's a penalty.

And don't forget, it's not compulsory to go round the keeper. If they leave a gap or don't come at you then put it in the corner or chip them. You won't see that open goal, but you'll still find the target.'

Bobby Charlton

'Today Ryan Giggs is one of the best in the game at going round the keeper to score. He's so quick. From my day, Jimmy Greaves was the master – what balance and vision.

For United, we had Denis Law and George Best. They were brilliant at it. But, for me, the best I've

It looks like a goal is on the way here if the man with the ball stays cool. The keeper has made his move and the player still has good control of the ball and is well balanced to sprint past to his left. The keeper remains capable of extending himself so the attacker must take a wide berth, but after that finding the net should be a formality.

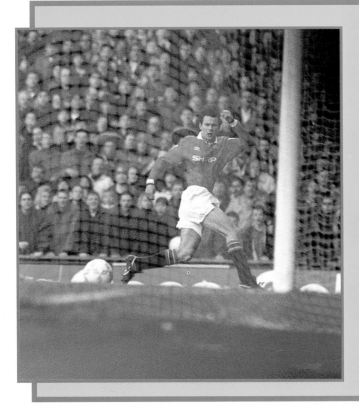

It's in, or is it?

If you go round the keeper cleanly, scoring should be a formality, but good keepers who are beaten at least make sure attackers are forced wide in the process. It means a striker, although clear, can be left with a difficult angle. Sometimes this means it's only at the very last minute you know your team's scored. Ryan's goal against Sheffield Wednesday in the Coca Cola Cup semi-final first leg (pictured here) had the crowd on their feet after he'd side-footed the ball goalwards. As you can see, the angle was really tight, and no one was sure if it was going in. It did, just, and was a crucial strike in giving United a slim 1–0 advantage to take to Hillsborough for the second leg which they also won, 4–1.

ever seen at rounding the keeper was Puskas. It's a while ago since he was playing for Hungary, but, even so, I can't remember him missing.

During my playing days, I never seemed to face the keeper on a one-to-one basis very often. But when I did it was no problem. It's just a dribbling skill really. Except you've got to give yourself more margin for error than against an outfield player. Remember, the one between the sticks can use hands!

It was no different than facing a really tricky full back. Like Ryan, I started my career at Old Trafford on the wing. I beat the keeper the same way; throwing a dummy and then using my pace. I'd try and get the ball on to the side from which I wanted to shoot, but there wasn't always time to set it up like that. I would if I could as it happens too fast for

the keeper to remember which way you are likely to choose. But whichever side, the goalie is in trouble and you're in charge. Stanley Matthews was brilliant at it. On the wing, he'd drop his left shoulder and go right. Up against the keeper it was exactly the same.

Keepers are getting quite good at making themselves a big target and the goals a small one. You've got to take advantage of the situation. The keeper's running forward and he has to be on his heels. All he can really do is spread himself.

If he does anything else you've probably got the chance to shoot. Okay, you haven't gone round the keeper then, but you've scored. Nowadays, more and more players try chipping the keeper. We'll deal with that later so you're fully equipped for your next one-on-one in the box.'

Dribbling

Speed and skill together are football's most potent combination; they get you past your man. Ryan has both skill and pace. Together, they make him one of the game's most feared attackers, and one of the most exciting to watch. Unless you're a full back.

Ryan Giggs

'Dribbling is exciting. The crowd at Old Trafford love it. They get behind you and give you a real adrenaline rush when you beat a player through skill and pace. As I usually play on the left wing I get plenty of chances to dribble. My job is to beat the full back and get a cross or shot in.

I don't have to be quick like an athlete over 100 metres. It's usually enough to sprint for 20 yards. If you're not that fast, don't worry. You can still get away by a change of pace. But if you are quick, then test your opponents every time you get the chance.

Keep the ball close to you – like Romario in the World Cup, or Spurs' Darren Anderton. The defender doesn't know whether to tackle or stand off if you have the ball at your feet. Then throw a dummy – drop your shoulder one way then go the other – or fake to pass. When the defender's taken the bait, go

When Ryan gets the ball, which way do you think he's going to go, left, right, or even straight ahead? It's a puzzler that Premier League defenders find themselves worrying about most weekends. Here you can see how Ryan shifts his weight to unbalance defenders. Ryan never lets the ball run away from him. That makes it very difficult for a defender to make a tackle as he can easily change direction quickly and keep the ball with him. Ryan is also always on his toes ready to change pace. When you've deceived the defender, you've got to be ready to go past and take advantage of the space behind.

the other way and attack the space behind them.

If the defender recovers, be ready for the tackle. Make sure your body is between the defender and the ball so you can block the challenge. If you're central and in the last third of the pitch, head for the penalty box. Once you are in there, it is risky for the defender to make a tackle. Good dribbling on the wing combined with pace gets you into the danger zone where a badly timed tackle means a penalty.'

Bobby Charlton 'Darren Anderton is quite fast and skilful. So is Romario. He seems to have the ball stuck to the end of his toe. But the best in Britain at running at speed with the ball is Ryan Giggs.

Ryan keeps the ball close and under control. It's a nightmare for defenders. They're on their heels and under pressure and the ball is too close to

When two players close you down, it's a real chance to make some attacking headway. If you get past them, it's like your opponents have been reduced to nine men. The player on the left is committed to a tackle. You can use this to your advantage as his forward lunge has left a zig zag path for you between the two of them. If you go right then left at speed, you should be away from them both. The second defender will be looking for you to have lost control so he can rob you. If you keep the ball close to you, you should be fine.

Ryan for them to rob it.

George Best was a great dribbler. He had balance. Defenders would try and knock him off the ball. He just shrugged off the challenge. Balance also helps the great players stay free from injury. They ride tackles: Pele, Maradona, Best ... and Giggs!'

The Match

What happens during the 90 minutes when Ryan Giggs is wearing the red shirt of Manchester United or Wales is the most important part of his life. He has to deliver on the pitch. If he doesn't, he won't stay on it for very long. Not surprisingly, Ryan is a bit on edge in the few moments before kick-off – 45,000 people in a stadium can have that effect on you.

'I just want to get on with it. At kick-off you get a tremendous rush of adrenaline. It helps when the crowd chant your name. They're brilliant at Old Trafford. It used to be worse when I was playing in district teams and for Manchester United's junior sides with about 200 watching. You can hear everyone then, your mum, your mates, anyone whose watching.'

An early goal does wonders for the confidence. As long as it's for United! 'If it's going well then half time is okay, but if things have gone badly ... The boss usually tells us to keep calm and keep trying to break the opposition down.'

When it works, all the preparation and effort, and care with diet and lifestyle, is worthwhile. If Ryan scores and United win, there's a real buzz. 'When you score, you just feel really happy.' But things don't always go to plan. Number 11 has his off days, even playing for the champions. 'The worst thing is when you're substituted. If you see the manager or Kiddo pulling your number out of the pile, you try and get the ball and beat five players before scoring! But if your number is up you've got to accept it's in the best interests of the team.'

Ryan suffered the season's first disappointment in only the second game of the new 1994/5 Premier League campaign. He was pulled off during a 1–1 draw with Nottingham Forest at the City Ground. Although at the time he looked really down when the manager called him off, it just made him more determined to make the new season his best ever for United and make it impossible for the bench to withdraw him again.

Playing on the wing, Ryan has a pretty good idea of how the bench think he's performing. 'I can hear most of what's being said.' If he's not having the best game of his life, the manager and touchline critics make sure Ryan knows about it, but he's been accused of having partial hearing when it comes to criticism from Alex Ferguson during a match!

On the pitch, there is plenty of encouragement. 'Because we've played together for a few seasons now, the team spirit at United is excellent. If one of us misses a sitter, no one blames him because he probably helped us win the game the previous week.'

Ryan loves playing at Old Trafford. Unfortunately, he can't say the same about Wembley, a pity as matches there are inevitable when you're as successful as Manchester United. 'I always seem to get taken off there.' Good games, back to back, in the FA Cup and Charity Shield have helped encourage a change of heart on the spiritual home of football.

The match is what really matters for Ryan. It's what he does on the pitch that's important. Old Trafford is known as the 'Theatre of Dreams' by the fans. It's Ryan's favourite ground in the Premier League, too.

Crossing

The cross comes in … it's there! How many goals have a commentator saying exactly that on television? Plenty, but without accurate crossing there wouldn't be a celebratory squeak out of John Motson and Co. just a groan from the crowd. As a winger, Ryan Giggs' main job is to deliver decent crosses. It's a part of his game that he admits he could improve on.

Ryan Giggs

'Alex Ferguson had me doing special work on my crossing when it wasn't going well during our second Premiership-winning season. It wasn't that I was incapable of crossing well, it's just that I was inconsistent. The special practice, with Brian Kidd, was just to help me take my time and make good contact, two aspects of crossing that are the key to ensuring a good supply of quality service to your team mates.

My problem was that I was rushing it and trying to hit the ball too hard. Kiddo took me aside after training had finished and told me where to hit the ball and how to make sure contact was smooth and not rushed. The quicker you hit the ball, the less accurate you are. Kiddo got me to take my time, even under pressure.

Kiddo also felt that I was trying to pick out players instead of aiming for areas of space that they could run into. This meant I didn't have much margin for error and the crosses became a bit too much 'all or nothing'. This is fine when you score from them, but it's a very difficult skill to master, picking out a single player for a cross. If it doesn't come off the good possession is usually lost. I was told not to take the risky option so often. Hopefully, I'm improving.

Ballooning the ball into the crowd is really disappointing because you know you can do better. It shouldn't happen, but sometimes it does – the ball bobbles or you take your eye of it – and it ends up with the keeper, either in the hands or spotted for a goal kick.

When you've got the chance to cross, you're looking for your strikers and midfielders running into the box.

Players like Alan Shearer are very good at getting between defenders and onto the end of a good outswinging cross. At United, big Dion Dublin is a good target for crosses – he's great in the air – while Mark Hughes is not the biggest player but gets

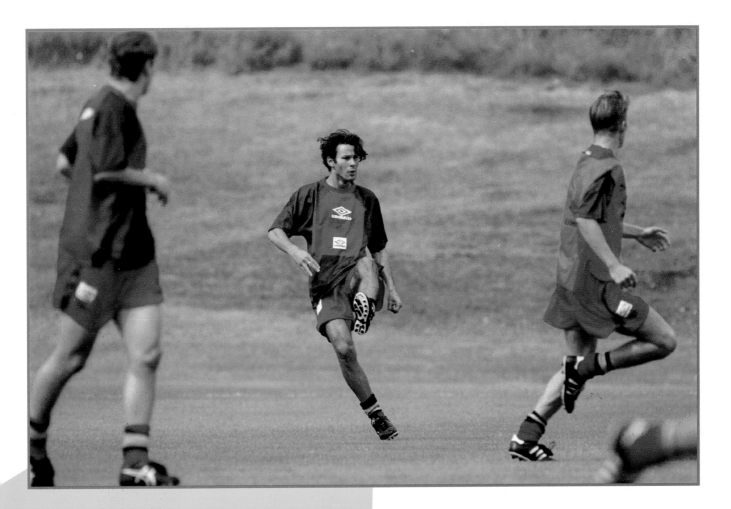

Brian Kidd (left) helped Ryan through a difficult patch with his crossing. This aspect of Ryan's game was inconsistent. Time spent on the training ground with such an experienced expert helped him. Kidd told Ryan to take more time when he was crossing.

You can see here how Ryan gets under the ball by leaning back . That's so there's some height when he is crossing. Having learnt to take his time, his crossing is much more accurate.

up well. Hughesy doesn't mind how it comes, really. If it's a bit low he has a tremendous volley as well as the ability to score with a diving header.

He scored a tremendous one against Liverpool in the season we won our first Premier League title. We were losing at Old Trafford against Liverpool 2–1 with only a few minutes left to claw back the deficit. I crossed from the left and Mark met it at the near post completely wrong footing Bruce Grobbelaar in goal. The cross was into the right area and Sparky did the rest to level the scores. Eric Cantona is also very good at getting on the end of crosses. He makes the bad ones look good.

Sometimes you haven't got the time to look for team mates. Then you have to hit into space, usually between the six-yard box and the penalty spot. That's tough for the keeper; he doesn't know whether to come for it or stay on the line. And defenders are chasing back for the ball. That's much harder to deal with.

The choice of cross is sometimes out of your hands. If the pass to you means you have to check your run down the wing then you'll probably have to supply an inswinger. If the ball is in front of you then the outswinger is on.

The quality of the ball your team mate gives you is crucial. A good ball means the attack doesn't lose any pace and the crosser doesn't have to adjust before swinging one in. It saves time.

The best ball is the one that gets you to the bye-line. From there you can cross for attackers to run onto. The midfield is coming through as well. If someone gets a touch, it can leave the keeper with no chance. If the ball you receive forces you to cut back, it doesn't mean the chance has gone. The extra time you have to take gives the midfielders the chance to arrive right on cue.

If I'm on the right, I might cut in to make my cross and use my left foot, but not every time. It's easy to defend against if you do the same thing over and over so I've worked on my right foot. It means I at least have the option of getting to that byeline when I'm on the other wing.

Full backs are going to be working hard to close you down on the wing, even if your team mate gives you quality possession.

If you're lucky, you'll know after a few minutes whether you've got the beating of your marker. If you have, then exploit it. Get to the byeline before crossing.

For me, there are no bad full backs in the Premier League. You can't take any of them for granted. They've all got something, pace, tackling strength, experience. Or they can be strong going forward. That means you've got to keep an eye on them when they have the ball.

Brian Burrows is an unsung full back who has a lot of experience and is tough to handle. Gary Kelly, the Leeds defender, is very quick. You have to outwit him. Even players with real pace struggle against him. Aston Villa's Earl Barrett combines pace and experience. He's very difficult to play against. But, as I said, they're all tough in the Premier League.

If the full back is making it difficult for you, your attackers can help sometimes. They can take some of the responsibility for cross selection. A shout from Mark Hughes – 'near post Giggsy' – and my mind's made up where the ball is going.

But I won't rush it. Not any more. You have to take your time and make good contact. Otherwise it's a waste.'

Bobby Charlton

'What Ryan says about crossing is exactly what we said about taking corners; make good contact, otherwise it's a waste.

It's hardly surprising, though. After all, a cross is just like a corner except the ball is moving. The same principles apply. You strike the ball to put spin on it so you can produce an inswinger or an outswinger, height or depth.

The crucial difference is that's much harder to cross! You have to hit a moving target. So, you have to practise even more!

If you are as quick as Ryan, you can get to the byeline. A cross from there is much harder to defend against as your pals are running onto the ball. Its pace helps them generate power. A quick glance is usually all you have time for to see where they are. But you don't want to be spending too much time measuring your cross. Just enough to get composed

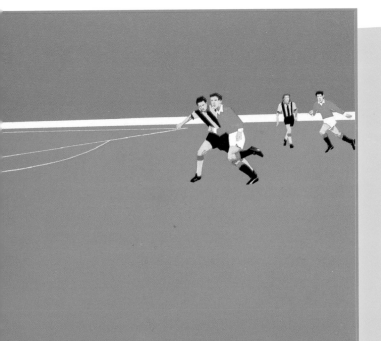

The defender who has closed you down has left two channels for a good cross; to his left – some swerve would help – into the path of the central attacker, or to his right, deep and high to the right winger charging in. If the defender closed you down any more, you would have to start thinking about going to the byeline as the angles left would mean the passes won't be an option. That would be easy, though. He's moving towards you and travelling in the wrong direction to cover. You'd have a head start on him down the line. The picture below shows how important balance and composure is to Ryan's crossing. Even though he's stolen a yard that gives him time to cross, he is under pressure from his marker and has to use his arms to keep steady as he shapes up to strike the ball. There is nothing illegal in this as long as Ryan doesn't push the opponent. The cross here was a floated outswinger. See the way Ryan leans back slightly to get underneath the ball to give it height as well as power.

and balanced. The sooner you whip it in the better. Defenders hate that quick outswinger. They have to hurry. That's when they make mistakes.

Keepers hate the inswinger. The ball is usually coming quite low and fast. It takes only a touch and its path is changed and suddenly you're celebrating a goal. Brilliant.

You've got to judge what sort of cross the keeper won't like. That's the skill of crossing. Not too near to the goal so the keeper can stay on the line and gather, but near enough to tempt the keeper to come for it, and miss it. You've got to assume the keeper is good and will catch anything too close to the goals.

But the keeper shouldn't really be on your mind. As long as you keep the cross a reasonable distance away from the goal, the keeper should not be able to come and claim it. If you're confident you can generate some power with your cross, you'll be able to go closer to the goal, but always bear in mind how much of a waste of good possession it is when the keeper intercepts the cross. As I've said, assume

the keeper is good and that a cross close to the goal will throw away some good attacking possession.

From my day as a player, Mike Summerbee was a great crosser of the ball for Manchester City. Your coaches will remember his outswinger. Today, I like the way Hagi puts the ball into the danger zone for Romania. The Dutch are very good at that; knocking into the penalty area for hungry forwards.

In the World Cup, the Swedes were excellent at crossing in balls for their big men – Kennet Andersson, for one – as they had the height advantage. But remember the Brazilians. They showed how important variety is in crossing. They don't pump in high balls because little Romario and Bebeto are two small lads. Their approach is different – but just as effective. Their crosses play to their strengths, low and into space.

The Brazilians never waste possession. Neither should you. Or Ryan! You mustn't waste an opportunity to get a cross in. Ryan's mentioned the full backs in the Premier League. Maybe they are better than in my day, but that's no excuse to waste

One of the world's best

Romanian World Cup star Gheorghe Hagi is one of the best crossers of the ball in football today and the outstanding footballer of his country's current generation. His skills have earned him close to a century of international caps and encouraged Real Madrid to sign him after some excellent performances at Italia '90. Sadly things did not work out in Spain and Hagi was transferred to the Italian side Brescia, but another good showing in the World Cup in America – Romania were quarter finalists in USA '94 – has seen him return to Spain, this time to play for Barcelona. Hagi is a great crosser of the ball with either foot. His strength is his variety. This makes it very difficult to plan a defence against him.

the ball. You can always check and bring the ball back on to your other foot. I find it very hard to understand how many crosses today hit the full back and go out of play – and not always for a corner. Forwards hate it when a good position doesn't produce a good cross. Stay composed. It's a waste otherwise.

Practising crossing is quite difficult. It may seem easy to arrange, but in reality, it's very difficult to recreate the pressure and speed of a match on the training ground. It's the pressure that makes you snatch at the ball and fluff the cross – or shot or pass – and that is always absent from the training ground and practice match. You've also got plenty of extra time away from competitive situations which makes it so much easier. The professional footballers you see make a hash of a cross in a match are all capable of delivering perfect service away from the tension of a game.

All you can do is make sure your general technique for striking the ball is fine and do your best to stay composed during the game. Remember, it's a moving ball so it's all the more crucial that the strike is clean. It means watching the ball more than

The attackers are close to being goal side of their markers for the cross from the left wing. It's very hard to pinpoint a cross but their movement encourages the early ball and shows the crosser what space they are going for. They can expect a winger at least to hit space, if not to land it right on their heads or perfectly at their feet. They are both still outside the box, so the cross should be well away from the keeper's reach.

ever, and following through to make sure you reach your team mates waiting for the cross in the box.

It's not the case that you have to land the ball on a sixpence. Pinpoint crossing is great, but trying to achieve perfect accuracy may mean you dwell on the ball just that moment too long and lose the opportunity. Crossing is about using possession to the best effect.

The ball into the space is the key. That's what your team mates want. Let them use their momentum to run onto the ball. It will help them generate power and that should mean strong shots and headers, and, fingers crossed, some goals.

After the Match

Footballers are sport's fastest washers. They're all out of the Old Trafford bath, dressed and ready to reflect on the 90 minutes with team mates, friends and fellow professionals in the players' lounge at least within an hour of the final whistle.

You'd think the mood would be dictated by the result – happy winners, downbeat losers – but it's not as straightforward as that. It can work the other way.

'Obviously, after the game we are normally a lot happier if we win, but when our 30-plus game unbeaten run came to end against Chelsea it was, in many respects, quite a relief.'

Ryan's own performance always affects him. 'If you've had a bad game, you think what you could have done better, but if you've won it's not that bad, although your form is always a concern.'

As a full international, Ryan often faces Wales team mates in Premier League games. He'll usually hang around a bit after the game to have a chat with them as well as any guests he's invited to watch.

'I'm not usually the last to leave as I like to get home and relax, but I'll try to say hello to international colleagues I've been up against or family and friends at the game.'

Home and relaxing means television. If he rushes on a Saturday he can catch the end of the Brookside Omnibus. A video of the week's Aussie soaps is an alternative if he's remembered to record them.

After some rest, Ryan may nip out locally with old friends. The movies are a popular option with team word of mouth usually being the deciding factor in what to see.

'I go to the pictures quite a lot. A few of the players are real movie buffs – Gary Pallister and Lee Sharpe go a lot – and if anyone has seen a good film they'll recommend it. I like Al Pacino and Robert de Niro in most things. My favourite films are *Goodfellas* and *The Godfather*.'

If there are a few days before the next game, Ryan sometimes takes the opportunity to go to a restaurant to unwind. The timing means he has the pick of the menu. There's plenty of time to recharge the carbohydrate stores before the next game. 'I can pretty much have what I like when I eat out because I don't put on that much weight. I

don't particularly enjoy desserts and prefer fruit but I might have the odd chocolate gateau – maybe on my birthday!'

The scales confirm this. Ryan put on the modest total of one pound in weight in the 1994 close season. He weighed in at an unworrying 10 stone 7 pounds for the start of another defence of the Premier League.

After a game, Ryan has earned some time away from the pressures of being a Premier League star for the champions, win, lose or draw. He's no different to most people in what he likes to do away from 'the office' – cinema, television, restaurants, just relaxing – and he likes to look the part when he is out and about in Manchester.

Of greater concern, sometimes, is good sleep after the match. This can be elusive after an evening game when the adrenaline has been pumping. 'Sometimes I'm still awake at 4am.'

Like most footballers these days, Ryan doesn't lose too much sleep over what appears in the sports pages. He's more worried about what the manager and his team mates think.

Through Balls into the Box

A decisive pass to a pal in the box who scores is as much a part of a goal as the shot that sends the ball into the back of the net. The dribbler who never needs to pass hasn't been born yet. Even Pele needed to receive good possession! As a forward, Ryan Giggs knows the value of a good through ball.

Ryan Giggs

'A good through ball makes my life easy. If Eric Cantona's got the ball, I know that, nine times out of ten, he'll find me in some space. It's frustrating sometimes on the tenth time when I don't get it, but that's part of being in the team. You can't expect the ball all the time.

At United, we all have our own preferences for the type of ball we like. Sharpey and Andrei Kanchelskis love the ball behind the defender. Then they can use their pace. Mark Hughes likes it to his feet. Now we've played together for a few seasons we know what each other likes. This helps a great deal. Learn your pals' strengths and play to them when you're passing into the box.

The one-two is a particularly good example of how effective a through ball can be into the box where it counts. Success here comes with teamwork and understanding which will develop over time. It has at United.

With most through balls into the box, I'm trying to get on the receiving end. It's different to when I'm out on the wing where my crossing makes me chief

The attacker off the ball here has made it very easy for you. He's caught your eye and told you he's running into the space between the two defenders closing you down. They've made a shot difficult, but there's plenty of space and time to thread a through ball into the box for your team mate to have a shot at goal. Communication has helped here. Your colleague hasn't given away an advantage by telegraphing his intentions as he's going to steal a yard on his marker. The defender knows where it's going, but there is little he can do about it. The shot on goal looks on.

A player capable of a good through ball has vision to see it and good technique to execute it. You can practise making a pass against a wall or in the park, but acquiring vision probably means spending some time away from the training ground watching football. This will help improve your awareness as a receiver, too. Whenever you're watching a match, keep an eye on players making passes into the penalty box.

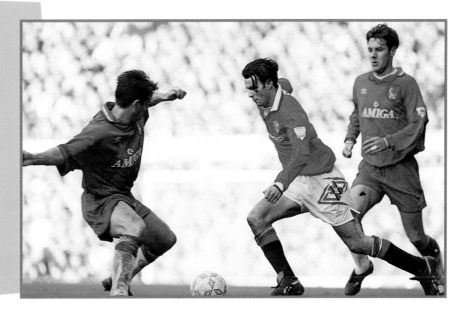

supplier. When I'm more central and moving into the box, my job is to make the passer's life as easy as possible by creating angles and staying onside. We'll cover that in the section about running off the ball.'

Bobby Charlton

'I played a quite a bit in midfield so a lot of the time I was the one threading the ball into the box for Denis Law and George Best to score. The technique's no different to striking the ball. Remember: watch the ball, strike cleanly through the centre, or hit the side if you want to bend it, or underneath for some height, and follow through. There's some more advice on passing (making good contact) coming up, too.

When you've got the ball in a dangerous position, like just outside the box, look for options. There might be a one-two on – Ryan's always looking for those. If not, you've got to find gaps in the defence where players are or into which they can run.

Talking all the time helps. You've got to communicate with your team mates. Even when you've not got the ball you should still be heard. Let your pals know where you think the space is. They might not have seen it. An opportunity to make a good through ball is too good to waste by keeping it to yourself.'

Man to Man

One-on-one is football stripped down to the essentials. It's just you against your opponent, a private battle. Players as gifted as Ryan Giggs sometimes find the opposition put a man on them with the sole intention of marking them out the game. The more skilful you become the more likely it is you'll have to cope with it, too.

Ryan Giggs

'The first time I was man-marked was at Notts County in only my second season in the first team at Old Trafford. Since then, it's happened quite a few times.

It's really important that you have a good game when it happens. Otherwise, you'll find teams always put a man on you. The manager gave me some good advice after I was man-marked for the first time. He made me think more about my game and what I was doing off the ball. It made me realize that sometimes you've got to sacrifice yourself for the sake of the team. You see, you can turn man-to-man marking to your advantage. If I'm being marked,

then that's one less defender for Mark Hughes to worry about.

By running off the ball you're able to take a man away from the danger zone. If he doesn't follow then fine; you've lost him and you're free to receive the ball. If he does then there's a good chance someone else will exploit the space. When there are two men

Ryan's shadow

Although Ryan is still relatively inexperienced in footballing terms, some clubs take the precaution of man-to-man marking him. For such a young player, this is a great compliment. The down side, though, is that Ryan is less free to express his skills during the match. But man-to-man marking is a problem all great players have to deal with. It means a lot of hard running trying to lose your marker. Even if you don't succeed, you'll still make space for others.

on you, even better, it means even more space.

It's hard work. It means lots of short sprints, twists and turns and changes of direction to throw the marker, but it's worth it. Once, against Aston Villa, they put a man on Eric Cantona for the whole game. We won and he scored twice! Man-to-man marking doesn't always work.'

Ryan was man-marked by Leeds full back Gary Kelly (above, on ground in white) on New Year's Day, 1994, at Old Trafford. It was one of the tussles of the season with honours ending with the visitor. Ryan took revenge at Elland Road in the return match, though, scoring United's second goal in a 2–0 win.

Bobby Charlton

'Being man-marked is very flattering. As a player, I didn't like it as I preferred to be able to find space and run around freely, but it's still a compliment that your opponents' manager is prepared to sacrifice one of his team with the sole task of stopping you getting the ball.

It's difficult, but you've got to dig deep and catch your marker dozing. You'll need stamina and the ability to change pace. Watch for when your marker's concentration is low so that you can take advantage of the lapse and enjoy some possession. Lots of twists and turns and dummies will do the trick. Confuse your markers. Wear them down.

I was man-to-man marked in the 1966 World Cup Final against Germany. In fact, it always happened to me against the Germans. Putting Franz Beckenbauer on me in '66 was an enormous compliment and I didn't mind. Even in the final. I knew our team was good enough to win without me so I worked to lose him and make space for others. It paid off. It may never happen to you in a World Cup Final, but it might in any big game for your team when you're playing familiar opponents who know how you play. Be ready for it.'

Chipping the Keeper

When it comes off, chipping the keeper seems effortless. The ball seems simply to float between the posts and under the bar, before gently nestling in the back of the net. It looks easy, but it's actually one of football's hardest skills to master. Excellent technique is needed. That only comes with patience and practice.

Ryan Giggs

'If it's a one-on-one situation, chipping the keeper is a last resort for me. It's better to go round the keeper than over the top as less can go wrong. If there is a gap, I'd shoot. If there's not, I'd use my pace. But if the keeper has closed down all the angles and has a good chance of robbing me should I try and sprint past, then I'll have a go.

It's difficult to execute a good chip in a match at pace, almost impossible to do it when you are running head on towards the goal at full pelt. You've got no angle to play with and the ball is running away from you. Unless you stop and check there's no way you can get under the ball to give it height. If you do that, then you've got the problem of another defender coming across. And checking means you've probably not been able to get into the penalty box where you have more protection from defenders running back.

But that said, if I'm running at an angle to the goal and the keeper has badly misjudged where he is in relation to his goal, I'll give it a go. I chipped Dave Beasant at Old Trafford when he was playing for Chelsea and the ball seemed to hang in the air for ever before missing the far post at the last minute. I think there was a gust of wind as I was sure I'd got it on target!

Lobbing the keeper is much easier to do on the run. The bouncing ball means it's easy to get underneath it. We won a game at Queens Park Rangers a few seasons ago when I lobbed our second after Incey had given us the lead with a great overhead. I was as well balanced and composed as

The keeper has made a bad error of judgement here. Although he has closed down the angles, he has come too far and will not be able to rob you before you shoot. The chip is on. The technique Ryan uses (see right) would be fine if you weren't so central. But as a head-on chip is such a difficult skill, you'd probably have to go either left or right – onto your preferred foot so you can strike the ball at an angle like Ryan is doing. It helps you get under the ball and get the height you need to clear the keeper.

he had been and knew it was in immediately. The only thing that worries me in situations like that is whether or not I've hit it too hard. Luckily, I knew I hadn't on this occasion as soon as I'd made contact.

I'll always practise my chipping because it's a very effective way of scoring in the right circumstances. It's never wasted time as you use the chip during a lot of attacking play anyway. By practising it for shots on goal, you'll also improve a useful skill for around the box when you're under pressure. Eric Cantona is a terrific user of the chip. He cuts a defender out of the game with it and the ball is behind the defence where it is really dangerous.

But, if you fancy scoring with a chip, you need vision; the ability to look up and see the keeper out of position. I reckon it's not really an option unless the keeper's at least ten yards off his line, but if you've got the confidence and feel composed, why not have a go? The keeper certainly isn't expecting it.'

Bobby Charlton 'One of
my old World Cup team mates, Martin Peters, was the best chipper of the ball I played with. He had the vision and the confidence to try it

when the chance was on. Today it's Ian Wright of Arsenal who stands out. He's got the confidence to try it and he's proved often enough that he is well capable of scoring with it.

It's an instant decision. It's like you're a gunslinger in the Wild West, you've got to act fast. Use that computer of yours. You know, the one on your shoulders. Make up your mind whether it's on quickly.

If you're as good at it as Peters and Wright then you should never be afraid to use your skill! It's the ideal way – skill permitting – of beating a goalie who has strayed off his line into no-man's land. In fact, it

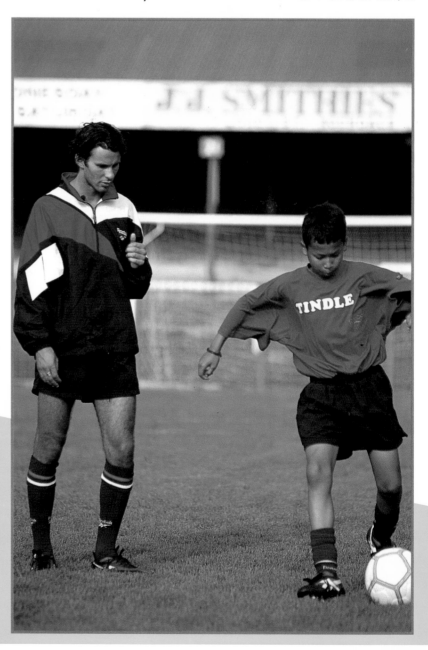

Chipping is much easier with a stationary ball than it is with a moving one. It is getting underneath the moving ball that is the problem. It's always running away from you. Check before you have a go otherwise you'll probably hit it straight at the keeper, and chip the keeper only when you're completely confident about it.

may be the only option you have. If the keeper is off the line quite a bit, then a lot of angles will be narrowed. A straight shot may not be on.

Composure is the key. As I said, you have to move fast, but not so fast you make a mistake. If you rush a chip, you probably won't score. Chipping is a very difficult skill so balance and a cool head become all the more important when you try it. Stay calm.

As Ryan explains, it's very difficult to do head on. You need an angle to get underneath the ball. It opens it up for you if you're left or right of centre.

Technically, it is no different to striking the ball

anywhere in the field. You've read the basics repeated over and over again. They're really important with this skill. Head down, good contact, a clean strike. You know the drill! But you may not feel you need necessarily to follow through here. If you're on the top of the box and it's a little chip with backspin you need, you'll just dig in behind the ball.

From further out, you can make sure the ball dips under the bar by putting some topspin on the ball. It's like a tennis shot that balloons up but drops in just before the baseline. You'll need to come over the top of the ball with your foot as you follow through to achieve this. Make sure you get enough height to clear the keeper, mind.

Topspin on a chip over the keeper is not for beginners. But with practice anyone should be able to learn it. You'll need a wall or a pal to practise with. If you've got both, then your pal can be the keeper and the wall's the goal.

If it's just a pal then he can stand where the goal would be and you'll just have to imagine where the keeper is. But I'm sure you can do that. With a bit of imagination, every chip is the winner at Wembley!'

Chipping the keeper like Ryan is here is not to be recommended in the last minute of the Cup Final. The skill is hard enough without adding the complication of some trickery. But even trying this cheeky chip, Ryan is still watching the ball and keeps his head still. The basic principles still apply. Good contact is vital.

Flicks and Tricks

Fans pay good money to watch football so, when the match situation permits, Ryan likes to entertain. Not when Manchester United are 3–0 down away from home. That's not the time to put on a show. When the hard work is done and the three points are safe. That's the time to party.

Ryan's got the skill for it. When he was breaking into the United first team as a teenager, Alex Ferguson said he was the most gifted individual of his age that he had ever worked with.

It is usually instinctive: 'I don't go into a game having decided to use a particular trick or skill, but if I'm in a situation that means I can use one then fine.

And if it comes off, then better still.' Sometimes Ryan stays on at The Cliff after training to perfect the twists and turns, back heels and flicks that set him apart from other players. He can balance the ball on the back of his neck, hold it between his calf and instep, even juggle while having a conversation, but only because he has perfected these moves on the

Practising tricks and skills is a fun part of training. No running or hard work. Ryan usually fine tunes his after the main session is over. He'll be ready when there's a chance in the match to show the crowd something special that he has perfected in private.

training ground. Tricks and skills are hard graft.

'Eric Cantona, Dion Dublin, Incey and Lee Sharpe often stay on after we have done the day's work for a skills session. They're great fun. The best juggler I've ever seen is Mark Walters' cousin. He's brilliant and even does it to raise money for charity.

A new trick I am trying to perfect is flicking it over the back of my head from between my heels, but it is quite hard. I can flick a bouncing ball over my head with my heel. That's not too hard to do and it's great when it comes off. The crowd love it. Once it's over your head, you're away. But the stationary ball is harder. I keep hitting my backside with it!'

One of Ryan's best tricks worked against Arsenal in a Premier League game at Old Trafford. It wasn't flash, just a clever way of taking out two defenders with one move. He dragged his foot over the ball a few times to the right then took his left foot round the outside of his right and flicked the ball between the pair. Or something like that. Even in slow motion

the commentator admitted: 'It is hard to see exactly how he does it.'

Ryan likes the way a trick or two lifts the spirits of the team. He admires other players who are skilful, as well. Sheffield Wednesday's Chris Waddle sometimes leaves him standing – or sitting. It's a bit much when the crowd are having a laugh at your expense and the grass is wet. But when it happens, Ryan's picking up new material! Next time, the joke will be on Waddle.

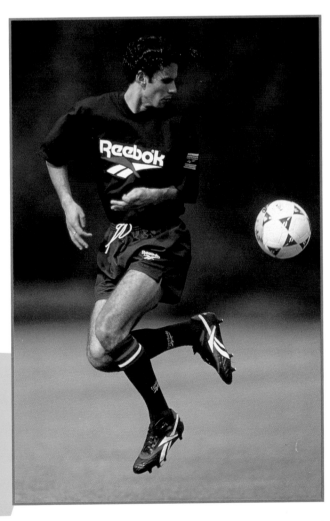

You can do all sorts of things with the ball if you practise. Some tricks though (left) are hard to work into the action of a Premier League game!

But, if you perfect your technique, there's no reason why complicated skills (right) cannot help you in a game. They're great for surprising defenders.

Volleying

Fans love to see the ball scream into the back of the net without touching the ground. If the striker makes good contact and it's either side of the keeper, it's a spectacular goal. But you've got to stay calm. Volleying is a difficult discipline. It's a tricky one to practise, too.

Ryan Giggs

'As a winger, I get plenty of opportunities to volley at goal. Crosses from the right come to me as I'm running to the far post if I've stayed on the left, or in the danger zone between the penalty spot and the six-yard box, if I've started my run from a more central position.

The flight of the ball determines whether the volley is on. That and conditions. If the pitch is bad, you'd be keener to volley than if you were playing on a good surface as the bounce is so unreliable. All this happens in a split second. You've got to focus on a volley very quickly and decide if it's on immediately.

Great to watch

A volleyed goal is always a real favourite with the fans; it usually flies into the net. Ryan got Manchester United off with a flying start to their Premiership retaining season with a volley against Norwich City in the first game of the 1993/94 programme. A headed goal mouth clearance saw the ball fall perfectly. Then, as Ryan shows here, it was a question of keeping cool, striking the ball cleanly, keeping it down and finding the target. All these aspects were present and correct at Carrow Road for the best start possible to a new campaign.

At United, we've got probably the best two volleyers of the ball in the country: Mark Hughes and Eric Cantona. I'm not bad at it, myself, but we all have to work at it. For me, that means more time with Kiddo on the training ground after the main session is over.

Andrei Kanchelskis got our 1994/5 season off to a flying start with a tremendous volley against Nottingham Forest at the City Ground. The cross came over from the left and Andrei steadied himself before catching the ball just right and putting it beyond the keeper into the far corner. He generated power as well as accuracy. It was a well-controlled volley. His balance was excellent, too, as he finished the shot with both feet off the ground.

I think what makes Mark Hughes such a great volleyer is his shape when he makes contact and the power he generates. Like Mark Hughes you must prepare to volley the moment the cross

Technique is crucial when volleying. Everything that holds with striking the ball is especially important with volleying. Here Ryan shows what a good follow through means. He's also still looking at the ball even though it's on its way to goal.

looks like it will fall kindly so that when it arrives you are perfectly poised. If you play golf, you'll know how important your shape is when the club head reaches the ball. Your shoulder should be facing in the right direction for a good shot. It's the same with volleying.

Sparky is perfectly shaped when he volleys because he's prepared for it. He's adjusted his body to volley. He's ready for it.

His power comes from technique. He doesn't try to knock the cover off the ball. It's timing again, like we said before about shooting, generally.

But power isn't everything. Direction is obviously important. It didn't quite work for Andrei last season. He struck one of the sweetest volleys I've seen in our top of the table clash against Blackburn when we were down and chasing the game, but it was straight at the keeper. The save was a quite straightforward reflex action. Sparky combines power with accuracy. It makes him the complete volleyer and guarantees some spectacular goals in a season.

I've put the ball into the stands or hit the corner flag with volleys a hundred times. That's why I have to keep practising my technique. It's a tricky one to work on though, volleying. Bobby's got some ideas on this, but it's very difficult to recreate the situation when you would volley. You really need a mate to feed the ball to you. Take it in turns, one feeds, while the other shoots.

Your practice should focus on making a good strike. For a volley, like everything else we've covered so far in this book, that means keeping your eyes on the ball and your head still. You've also got to keep your balance. It helps here if you use your arms to steady yourself. You don't want to miss and fall over. Apart from the embarrassment factor, you could get injured on landing.

Keeping the ball down is also important. Good contact isn't much good if the ball's gone over the crossbar. You can keep it down by making sure you hit the top half of the ball on impact. It helps to get your body over it.

The half-volley – taking the ball as it bounces – is no different to the full-volley, except, perhaps,

Here, the volley is your only real option. The defenders are going to be on top of you in a second (in a similar situation below, Ryan has just shot and the defender has made up the ground in an instant) and the ball isn't dropping fast enough for you to have time to control it before shooting. You've got to act fast to take the chance. But if you make good contact, you'll probably score. You are close to goal and the keeper has left a gap. So it's perfect for the volley. You are fully justified in having a go. With defenders so close, concentration is crucial. Don't be put off. Keep balanced and watch the ball. The follow through will give you the power.

that it's even more crucial to get you body over the ball on contact. From in the box or close range, players often favour a half-volley as generating power is less crucial, but it is vital you are over the ball, particularly if you're side footing it. Meeting the ball on the bounce is hard enough to time without wasting the chance because you weren't over the ball.

Half-volleys and full-volleys are worth all the effort, though. Great to watch, great to score.'

Bobby Charlton 'Ryan's right to go on about practice. You can't get enough where volleying's concerned. You can practise on your own, though. If you put a ball in a string bag, or like

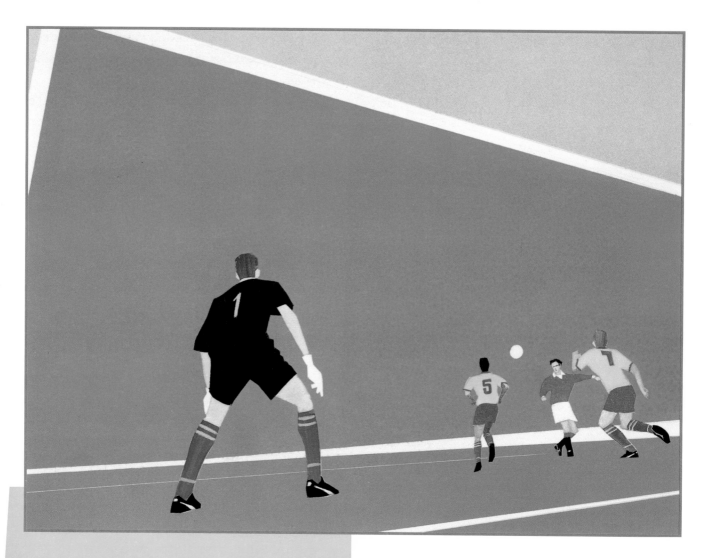

The keeper is going to struggle if the shot here is accurate. He's left a gap at his near post. In this situation, it's worth sacrificing some power for accuracy as there's the space to exploit. If there was a bit more space, a side-footed volley might be the best option, but with the defenders closing in, it's better to take it on the full.

us, use a 'Soccerpal', you can get confidence in your ability to strike the ball and perfect your technique. It'll mean you're ready for when the ball really is coming to you through the air from a cross.

The ball in the bag can go almost anywhere with you. Take it out on a walk. The odd kick here and there will get you used to the ball in the air. In time a volley should become second nature.

Volleying is so exciting to watch, it's got to be

worth all the effort and time practising. It's instantaneous and unexpected, you can generate such power, and for professionals and fans, alike, it means great pictures in the papers!

You can look an absolute fool if it goes wrong which is why some players don't try it. They'll let the ball bounce or take time to control it before getting a shot in. But those few extra seconds mean the chance may be snatched away by a defender. You'll lose the element of surprise, too. A good volley can catch keepers on the hop. It's goal-bound so quickly, it's very difficult to react to.

I know Ryan's already nominated him, but you can't avoid mentioning Mark Hughes when you're talking about great volleyers. He plans ahead and if he does look acrobatic when he scores, its because that is the shape he has to be to score from the cross. He's not being flash, it's just the best way to score. The path of the ball dictates where you must be and if that's in the air....

The overhead kick – the most exciting of volleys – is a very good example to illustrate this. The only way the striker can make contact with the ball behind his head is by attempting a demanding piece of gymnastics in its own right. Paul Ince's goal in the Charity Shield showed this. The ball was out of reach for him to try a normal volley so he had to try a bicycle kick. He did it to score, not to impress the judges.

There's no doubting Paul's goal was a great strike. But most good football works because it's so simple. The volley is no different. You don't get extra points for making things more complicated. The volley is a tough one anyway without adding ant frills unless you have to. Although some players do volley the ball when they're passing, I can't recommend it. Away from the box, there should be more time and space. And unless you're closed down very quickly, there should be time to bring the ball down.

It makes sense really. Technically the volley is a difficult discipline, so the benefit from it has to be large enough to take the risk. A centre half I played with made this point to me very early in my career at United. I'd given away possession with a volleyed pass and he wasn't at all pleased. He took me to one side when there was a break in play later, to tell me he didn't lose teeth and sweat blood to win that ball for me just so that I could give it away by volleying.

I got the message. But volleying's fine in the penalty box. Taking a chance is all right for a goal. It's not a natural thing so the hard work has to be put in, though. Even superstars like Mark Hughes practise. The whole United team will on the Thursday and Friday before a game: half-volleys, volleys, finishing.

You can never stop improving your technique, applying the basic principles that we've already talked about. They're worth repeating again, particularly when it comes to volleying. If you forget to keep your eye on the ball, you'll never score with

a volley. If you're unbalanced, an attempt to volley will get your team mates groaning as you'll never hit the target.

Like any shot, it's important to get the balance between power and accuracy right. No prizes for hitting the cover off the ball. It's a tough discipline and the basics apply to volleying, perhaps more than any skill. Keep practising them and you'll be fine.'

Volleying is all about confidence. If you're happy with your technique then you'll go through with the shot expecting a goal every time . Putting a ball in a string bag to practise striking it off the ground is a good way of improving your technique so that you won't be afraid to volley in the match when the chance to score comes to you in or around the box.

Heading

Bobby Charlton was never a great header of the ball. Ask him! But he scored in the European Cup Final with a header. And a few times for England. Ryan Giggs has scored some crucial goals with his head, too. He may not be the tallest player in the league, but he'll still get on the end of a cross to score, ever since his first one in 1992 against Nottingham Forest. United won the Premier League that season. The bump on the head was worth it.

Ryan Giggs

'So you don't think you can head the ball, do you? It might hurt? Well, if you head the ball correctly it won't. It's as simple as that. Bobby will tell you the same. He used to worry about his head and then the penny dropped; head it correctly and you'll be fine.

You've got a head start on Bobby. It took him a while to get it right. You can get it right now. It's all about confidence – like penalties! If you concentrate on heading it correctly and keep your eyes on the ball so you make contact with your forehead, then you'll hardly feel it. And you'll get power.

Don't let it hit your head. It'll be like a hammer hitting you into the ground. That would hurt! Attack the ball. Imagine it's an old boyfriend or girlfriend!

Remember to keep your mouth closed, though. If it's open, your tongue can pop out when you jump. You could give it a nasty nip when you land.

My first header at Forest was a low one. I could have got my foot to it, but I decided to head it and get off the mark. It's great to score your first header. It was no different for me.

I mainly have to make attacking headers. This usually means heading it down. It's hard for the keeper to stop it if it's low and in the corner. You can head it up if you think it's more effective, but

Watch the ball, but don't use your hands! Here Ryan has the ball exactly where it would be for an attacking header (without the finger as support!). Keeping your eyes on the ball is crucial for that good contact needed to give the combination of power and accuracy for a header on goal. In attack, Ryan would probably head down as it's much harder to save. He's poised to make contact with his forehead, leaning into the ball. It means he heads the ball, it doesn't hit him; he gets power and he doesn't get hurt.

get underneath it and it can go over the bar. Headers are hard to control.

The best headers of the ball are thinking about it long before they actually have to make contact. It's no different from when you're attacking from corners. You've got to try and make space and when it comes at head height, get on the end of it. Good headers are on their toes, looking for space, ducking and diving, getting ready to make a decoy run, maybe.

Timing's important. Don't make your burst for space too early. I'm not big enough to beat most centre halves in the air, but I can make space and get a free header in if I move at the right moment – when they're off balance. Go to the near post, or check and go to the far post. Use your head – literally. If you're on the end of a cross, an outswinger, head the ball in the direction it came, into the corner, if you can. The keeper will be following the flight of the ball when the cross comes in. A header in the opposite direction and they haven't a chance if it's on target.

(Left) The cross is coming over, but you've still got to get between the man and the ball. It's probably the case that the number 3 is a bit taller than you as he's a defender, so it's all the more important that you get in front of him and make contact before he does.

Ryan doesn't score that many goals with his head but strikes against Everton (above) and Oldham (right) were two which helped Manchester United retain their Premier League title. The goal against Everton was a great example of Ryan's speed helping him against defenders who are taller than him. He just nipped in front of them.

Inswingers are different. Then, just a touch will be enough. You're using the pace and spin of the ball against the keeper. A little deflection is very hard to defend against. Turning your body will help in directing the ball. Your neck's where the power comes from. Attack the ball. Don't be afraid of it.'

Bobby Charlton 'So many young players I have come across in all the time I've been coaching tell me they can't head the ball. It's always the same. It hurts. But, by the end of the session, they are all heading it fine. With a bit of practice,

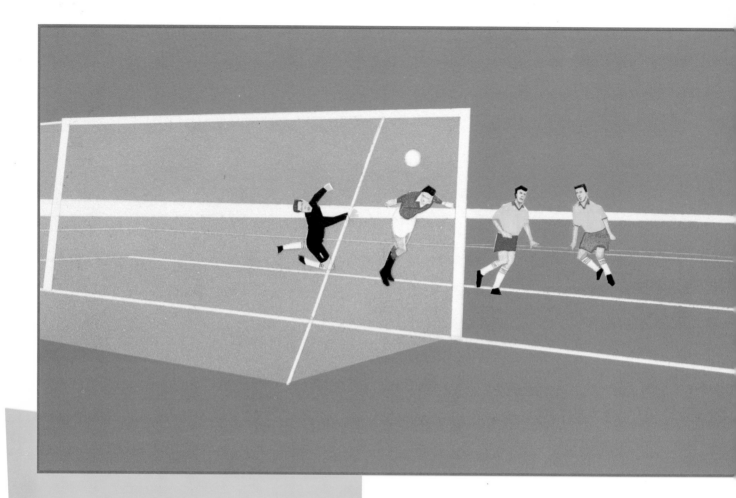

The striker has met the ball brilliantly here. The defence has been caught napping and from this close range the keeper had no chance. All that was needed was good contact. But it's no accident that the hero has ended up in such a good position. He has judged the path of the cross ahead of his marker and lost him with a quick burst of pace. You don't need to be the fastest player on the pitch to manage this. Playing with your team mates means you develop an understanding of where they are likely to cross. This puts you at an advantage over the defenders. This can be exploited to the full with a goal.

they've got another skill to take into the match with them. They don't think they can head the ball, but it is usually the case that they can. They're just using the wrong technique. When we've sorted out the correct method, it doesn't hurt anymore and the confidence comes. After that, there is no stopping them, they are heading it all the time,

even goal kicks.

I got the hang of it eventually! Heading was never a strong part of my game, but I was much more comfortable in the latter part of my career. I used to score, all right, and a fair few important ones at that, but I was never confident in the air. I always used to admire the players who could head the ball dropping from a goal kick. By the end of my career, I could do it, no problem.

I wasn't as good as some of the people playing in my day, though. John Charles could head as well as taking those powerful free kicks that made us turn our backs on him in the wall. Bolton's Nat Lofthouse was another. I never saw him play, but I was told that Tommy Lawton was a great header of the ball, too. They said he used to fly.

It doesn't matter if you're small. Good timing can mean a smaller player winning the ball in the air ahead of a taller man. It's your spring. Good jumpers are on the way up for the ball when others are on the way down.

If you watch today's professionals heading the ball – the Gary Pallisters and Steve Bruces – you'll see they never take their eyes off the ball. That's the key to good heading.

It won't hurt if you concentrate on the ball. You're too engrossed to feel anything and you're much more likely to make contact with the hard part of your head – the forehead. You can build up confidence on your own by heading against a wall. If you and your pal are both anxious to improve your heading technique, it's good fun to see how long you can keep the ball up using your heads. A third friend can be the 'piggy in the middle', but you'll have to be quite good to play that game.

Playing these games is a good way of practising defensive headers. With these it doesn't matter so much how accurate you are; power and distance are more important. You've got to get underneath the ball to give your fellow defenders time to get clear of the danger zone. Head the ball up. While it's in the air it's not with the opposition causing trouble.

All that's left is the diving header. That's for the very brave – like Mark Hughes. When they go in, they're brilliant. It's well worth learning to head well to score one of these. Don't wait until you've been playing for as long as I had before you work it out.'

Eyes down

Never be afraid of the ball when you're heading. If you are it will hurt. If you're not, it's no different to kicking the ball, and that doesn't hurt your foot. (At least , it doesn't if your technique is right.) Attack the ball, make contact with your forehead and keep your eyes focused on it. That will stop it hurting. Ideally you want to meet the ball at the peak of your jump, like Ryan has here. That way you make the most use of your height. If you're not that tall, don't worry. If you time your jump better than the defender marking you, you'll cancel out the natural advantage against you.

Playing for Wales

Englishmen are united in regret over at least one footballing issue: Ryan Giggs was born in the wrong country. Each cap Ryan wins for Wales is a painful reminder of talents that are denied to the country where he now lives.

The regret is heightened by the fact that Ryan played for England Schoolboys. Indeed, he captained them against Wales at Swansea in a 5–1 victory for his temporarily adopted flag. 'When I made my debut for Wales Youth I wasn't very popular!'

If this all seems a bit confusing, it's easily explained. The rules mean you have to play schoolboy football for your country of residence, but after that it's your blood that's important. And Giggs is 100 percent Welsh.

'I was born in Wales and most of my family still lives there. I am Welsh through and through, but there was no way I could play for Wales at schoolboy level.'

Giggs didn't have to wait long to represent the Red Dragon for the first time. In fact, his senior international debut wasn't that far away, either. He came on as a substitute against Germany aged 17 years and 321 days. It meant he has had the opportunity to play with some of his true footballing heroes, Neville Southall, Ian Rush, Dean Saunders, and of course, Mark Hughes.

Ryan loves representing his country. Cardiff

He's got the lot

After Ryan made his full debut for Wales, Kevin Ratcliffe, his captain with over 50 caps to his name joked: 'Now I can tell my children I've played with Ryan Giggs.' Another former international, Brian Flynn, who coached Giggs with the Wales Youth team and is now manager at Wrexham adds: 'He's got the lot. Balance, pace, timing, temperament. When I first saw him in a training session I could tell. I thought he'd be in the full squad within two years.' Flynn believes Ryan Giggs is the best football player he has ever seen. Quite a compliment.

Arms Park, where the national team play big games, is his favourite ground, along with Old Trafford. He enjoys the away games, too.

'The travel is great. You don't always get a chance to see much of where you are playing, but it's great to play against the European teams. It's a lot different to playing in the Premier League.'

Giggs nominates his first goal for Wales as his favourite career strike. It was in a crucial World Cup qualifier against Belgium in March 1993, the first game that he started, at a packed Arms Park.

'To score was fantastic. We hadn't started the group very well and it seemed to kick us into life.'

It's one of Giggs' few career regrets that Wales missed out on the '94 World Cup after losing against Romania in what proved the decisive match of their group.

'Getting to the World Cup with Wales is something I'd love, and there's the European Championships in 1996 in England. We have a difficult qualifying group, but hopefully we can

Cardiff Arms Park is where Wales play rugby union internationals. Although the home side has seen some lean years there lately, the atmosphere still makes playing at the Arms Park an ambition. The Football Association was granted permission to stage internationals there as well.

come through.'

Ryan and Wales will face Germany, Bulgaria, Georgia, Albania and Moldova in their struggle to get to the Euro '96 final stages. Their last game is away to Albania. The highlight of the group, a home game against Germany is in October 1995. The last time the two teams met, Wales pulled off a shock 1–0 win. A repeat would be a great help in this tricky group in which Wales will start as third favourites behind World Cup stars Bulgaria and, of course, Germany. Whatever the outcome, Ryan is sure of visiting some exotic places with Wales.

The One-two

The wall pass, the give and go, the one-two – three different names for one very effective way of getting the ball behind the defence. Using a pal is so much safer than trying to dribble round an opponent. If this move is executed properly, you'll get the ball back in a much better position than when you first passed it. And it's so simple: give and go. Easy, and probably the reason why Ryan Giggs uses the one-two so much when he's playing for Manchester United and Wales. Whichever red shirt he is wearing, the one-two means defenders are more likely to end up seeing the number on the back than the badge on the front.

Give and go

The one-two is simplicity itself. If it works, you're away and there's nothing the defender can do about it except watch you speed off into the danger zone. Here, Ryan has passed and is about to run on for the return. The defender has already moved to tackle the receiver. If the return ball is good, Ryan is away. The one-two worked brilliantly for Manchester United in 1994 against Leeds at Elland Road as the championship reached a climax. Ryan gave the pass and Mark Hughes acted as the 'wall'. The return ball was perfect and Ryan ran on into the box to score. That sort of understanding with your team mates comes from playing together over three seasons for United and Wales.

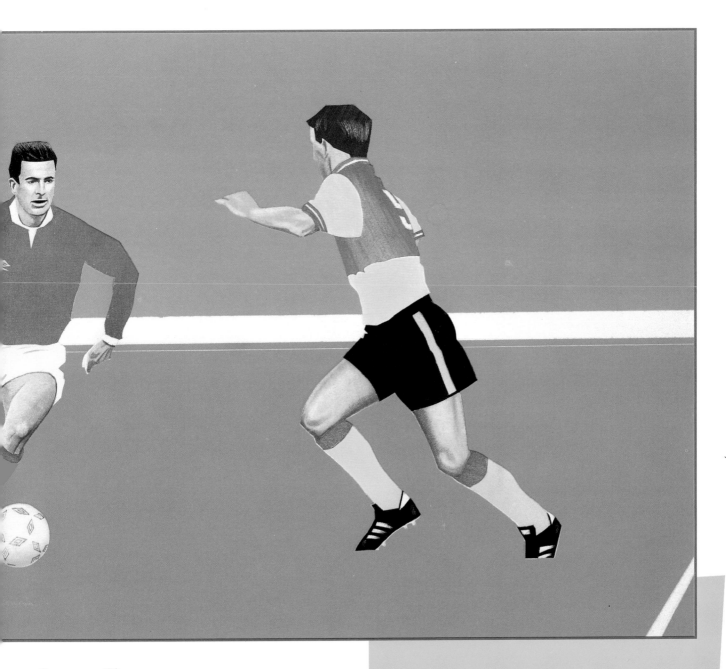

Ryan Giggs

'At United, we've got plenty of pace in our attack – Andrei Kanchelskis, me and Sharpey – and players who love to get forward, like Incey and Roy Keane. We're all lucky that we're in the same team as Eric Cantona and Mark Hughes. They're both brilliant for playing one-twos with when there's not very much space and you're under pressure.

Technically, the one-two is very straightforward. If you start with the ball, it's just a short pass and then a sprint to get on the end of the return ball. If you're the wall, like Eric and Sparky, then it's just a case of a

The defender has spotted that your team mate is considering a pass to you and has moved to close you down. If the pass comes quickly, the defender will be out of position to pick up your colleague so the return pass will be very effective; it's taken one man completely out of the game.

good return pass – accurate and well weighted – to run on to.

The more successful we've become at United, the more important the one-two has become. Sometimes, one of us will have two players marking us, so being surrounded by players who you can play the one-two with means we don't get shut out of the game.

It's particularly effective just outside the box. It's this area where space is in really short supply when I'm being marked. If a one-two is on and it comes off, there's a good chance that the move will finish with a shot. It's great for beating a full back, too.

It can mean important goals in important games when space is tight. In the run in to our second championship, we had a tough game away against Leeds. I was lucky enough to score our second goal in a 2–0 win after a great one-two with Sparky just outside the box. It left Gary Kelly, who was marking me, a couple of yards behind.

It works in any part of the field. All it needs is two team mates and one opponent. The player without the ball has to make the angle, and then, as long as the control and passing is good, you're away. It's impossible to defend against. And it's safer than dribbling.'

Bobby Charlton

'Ryan doesn't usually need to use a wall pass. He's a pretty good dribbler! But, as he points out, it's safer than taking the man on, and Eric Cantona's a pretty good wall.

So are the Brazilians. When he gets near the box, that man Romario again is looking for a quick give and go. It's a defenders' nightmare. They want you facing away from goal. The one-two sees you running at them head on. They're outnumbered and, before they know it, the ball's behind them in the danger zone. If you're the wall, you've got to be on your toes and making an angle. Whoever's marking you will try and make it difficult for you. You've got to adjust your position to help the attacker.

When your pal gives you the ball, use your computer – that one in your head! – and weight a pass back that is something to run on to. Just help it on its way, first time if you feel confident. With good timing, it's impossible to stop.

If you're the one with the ball, it's a terrific

If the ball is delivered immediately here, the one-two is definitely on, and it's going to give the give-and-go half of the move a route into the box if the return pass is accurate. That means it must be weighted perfectly and the passer must anticipate where his team mate is going to run and when he will arrive there. The above training routine is an excellent way of improving your technique for the sort of pass that's needed for one-twos near the box where space is tight. A few players make a circle and then two volunteers are 'it' and have to try to get a foot on the ball either by tackling or interception. You'll have to pass quickly and accurately if you want to avoid becoming the 'piggy in the middle', and it will prepare you for the give-and-go situation on the left.

advantage if you've got a bit of pace – it'll carry you right away. But it doesn't matter if you're slower than the defenders. That's what's great about the wall pass. You'll still definitely be able to get past them. The only way you can come unstuck is bad passing.

This one's very easy to practise. If you're on your own then find a wall and try running alongside and passing against it. Two of you means one can pretend to be a defender while the other uses the wall to go past him, just like in a match.

If there's three of you, one can be the defender and the other two can work at keeping the ball by using angles to pass. If there's more, even better. The angles are better and it's more fun. Whoever's in the middle stays there until they get a foot on the ball. This situation – plenty of bodies in a confined space – is a bit like midfield. It's in midfield that the give and go can also be effective as well as down the wing and just outside the penalty box, as Ryan's already mentioned. Dribbling's tricky. Only the best do it well. You can all give and go.'

Tackling Back

Tackling's part of the game. It's rough and tough and sometimes you get hurt, but there's plenty of skill involved. The more skilful you are, the less likely it is you'll get injured. As an attacker, Ryan Giggs does most of his tackling chasing back. Just because he scores the goals, he doesn't shirk his responsibilities.

Ryan Giggs

'It's not a great deal of fun, tackling, but I always try to get the ball back if I lose it. It's important. The crowd and your team mates should know that you'll always do the work for them when the situation requires it. It's good for team spirit.

When I started playing in the first team for Manchester United, I don't think I was strong enough for the tackling. Maybe that's why the manager played me on the wing. If you're not yet big and strong, don't worry. I trained hard and grew and now I can do it. You'll be okay, too.

Timing is the key to good tackling. This is really important now that the rules have changed about tackling from behind after the World Cup when the regulations were tightened up. You've got to make sure you play the ball and don't foul the opposition – even if it's an accident.

Keep your eye on the ball. How many times have we said that! But it's really important in tackling.

Timing is the key

The World Cup in America saw the introduction of new rules about tackling from behind. These were adopted by the Premier League. The changes mean that players making contact with their opponents when tackling from behind will be booked. As Ryan does a lot of tackling back it's even more important now that his challenges are well timed. Too early or too late and he'll get the man before the ball and end up with a yellow card. Here Ryan has timed his tackle well. You can see he's watched the ball and not the man and, as a result, made clean contact.

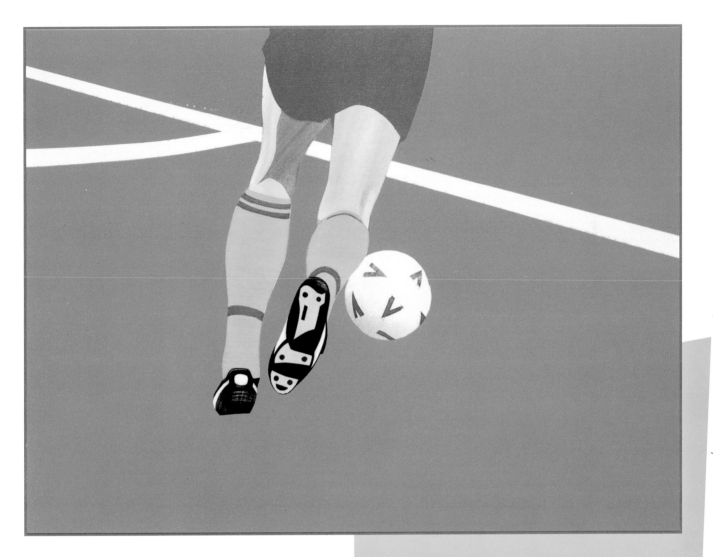

Unless you do, you may catch your opponent and then it's in the hands of the referee. And you've still not got possession even though you've made the effort to win the ball.

My advantage is my speed. I can catch up on whoever has robbed me quite quickly. But speed isn't all there is to it. Surprise is just as important. If you can sneak up on the full back who's just robbed you and catch them napping, you can pinch the ball back without turning a hair. Then tackling is enjoyable!'

Bobby Charlton

'Serious tackling's not for youngsters, really. It's for when you're older and stronger and are playing competitive football in a league. If you're learning tricks and improving your skills, then don't worry about it too much, for now.

I was never the greatest tackler, myself, even at

There's not much of the ball for you to aim at here. That's what makes tackling back so difficult. You are behind and a direct path to the ball is blocked. Your opponent in possession is shielding the ball. A good tackle back here is going to have to come from the right, but be careful not to trip your opponent.

the end of my career. In the United team, we had some great tacklers, like Nobby Stiles. But I always did my fair share of chasing back. My defenders told me not to worry too much about winning the ball as long as I got between the man with it and the goal. When Ryan started it will have been the same for him. If you're not built to be a great ball winner, at least make yourself useful.

For now, though, let's improve your skills. There'll be plenty of time for tackling later!'

Running off the Ball

When managers tell you you've got a 'good engine', they don't think you've got a car! It means they think you're a good worker, as well as being skilful. You can run all day, chasing back and making tackles. But, if you're an attacker, it's important where you run as well as for how long. Forwards do most of their hard work when they haven't got the ball. Great teams have strikers and wingers who are constantly moving off the ball.

Ryan Giggs

'When the manager talks about running off the ball to me, he really means moving. It's no use just running up and down the wing. I wouldn't be very dangerous doing that for Manchester United. I'd be predictable and easy to mark. Running off the ball means making angles and making space for team mates to exploit.

It's not just me. We all have to run off the ball. We have to give options to the player with the ball.

It's not always noticed, either. You have to wait

Running off the ball can be a thankless task, particularly if your team mates don't pass to you after you've sprinted the length of the pitch. But even without the ball, you are unsettling defenders and worrying the opposition by taking up dangerous positions.

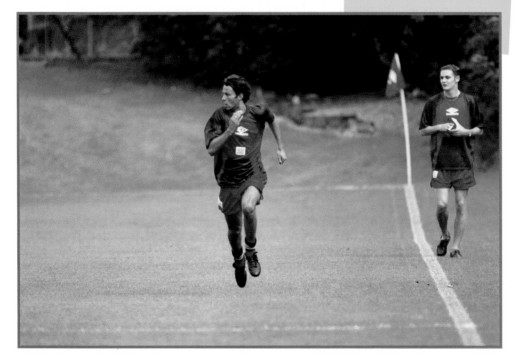

for the pat on the back if your decoy run made some space for a pal to score. But the effort is worth it if the ball ends up in the back of the net.

At United, we play through midfield so I'm not usually making my move up front too early. Sometimes if Gary Pallister's got the ball in defence and he sees me free he'll drop it in behind the full back and I can run onto it. It's not the norm, but I've got to keep my eyes open for it.

It's more likely to be a shorter pass, a little chip or a swerver with some spin. This means it's a lot of

Your team mate on the ball has two options: to pass to you on the left or to pass inside to another colleague. Although there is no guarantee you'll get the ball, you've still got to put in the effort by running down the wing as you'll probably take with you the defender who is putting your colleague under pressure. The defender will have to go with you, just in case you do receive a pass.

There is plenty of space on the wing (above) and the defence is outnumbered two to three. It's a situation that should be exploited. That means hard running (see Ryan really dig deep below in an effort to make himself available for a team mate) and plenty of work on behalf of the team. Football is a team game and running off the ball is all part of it. The last thing you want is for people to mutter that you are interested only in scoring yourself. In this situation the winger would probably be rewarded for his effort with the ball as he has got a clear run to the byeline and the chance to cross. By then the player who started with possession or the central striker will most probably be in good positions to get on the end of a testing centre. As the defence will be chasing back, there is a good chance that the attack will end in something substantial: a goal.

short sprints. It's all about vision, you and your pal seeing an opening. There isn't really any way you can practise it, it comes naturally or with experience through watching football and playing games.

What you can work on is your fitness. If there are five minutes to go, you need to be able to keep making the runs. Experience helps. You must use your brain when you're running. You don't want to be tiring yourself out on wasted runs off the ball.

It's all about making sure you're going to get into the right position to use those skills that you've learnt.'

Bobby Charlton

'The British game of football is all about hard work. We run hard for the whole match and extra-time if necessary – England's record in matches that have gone to an extra half hour is excellent – and professionals have to go through the pain barrier.

They'll always push themselves in the last five minutes of a match.

But running off the ball and hard work, as Ryan says, are two different things. The Dutch team of the 1970s, with Johan Cruyff, did a lot of running off the ball, but they were a skilful rather than a hard working side. The current Manchester United team is the same. The difference is that both these teams run off the ball to create things with purpose. It's the sort of running that causes the defenders problems, pulling them out of position and making space for others to score.

For now, you should be concentrating on your skills, enjoying the game. But when you watch football, keep an eye out for the hard worker, the one who makes the decoy run. When the time comes and your football is really competitive, it will help you. You'll go through the pain barrier, without wasting your energy if you do.'

USA '94

The World Cup in America was widely rated as one of the best ever in the competition's history. For Ryan, it was memorable, apart from the football, as it marked his on-air debut and because he was able to eat in restaurants in Los Angeles for a weekend and not get recognized!

'Reebok, whose kit I wear, flew me and a pal out to see their headquarters and to California for the final at The Rose Bowl. It was nice having to sign only a few autographs, although I don't mind doing them and try not to turn anyone down. I commentated on the final at The Rose Bowl for ITV which I enjoyed.'

Television's newest – and youngest – soccer pundit also enjoyed seeing Romario and Baggio, two players he admires greatly for their skills, both reach the final. 'I watched a lot of the football as you can learn different things. There seemed to be so many good games, it's hard to pick one out. I enjoyed all the Brazilian games. They were so good going forward. They keep the ball well and their passing is so accurate and first touch so good.'

From the point of view of his own international career, Ryan was disappointed that Wales failed to make it to the USA. It prompted further comparisons with George Best who, as a full international for Northern Ireland, never performed on the ultimate footballing stage during his playing career.

Ryan took heart from the performance of Romania and Belgium, the two eventual qualifiers from Wales' group – they both got to the quarter-finals – but did feel the odd pang of envy while the tournament thrilled spectators and television audiences alike for a month. It is every player's ambition to play in a World Cup and Ryan is no different.

'I enjoyed seeing Romania and Belgium do well as they were responsible for knocking us out, but it

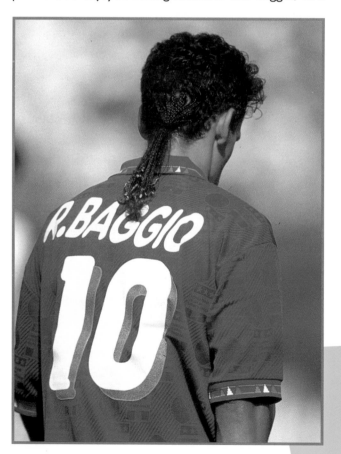

Roberto Baggio missed the decisive penalty for Italy in the World Cup Final shootout which handed the trophy to Brazil, but he is still one of the stars from USA '94 that Ryan admires.

COL 0:45 ROM

*WorldCup*USA94

The Rose Bowl, Pasadena, was the venue for the 1994 World Cup final. Ryan was there as a television pundit for ITV, along with more than 90,000 fans.

Romario wasn't the captain of World Cup winners Brazil, but he, more than anyone, deserved to hold the trophy after scoring five times in the competition.

was quite tough seeing them play as you couldn't help thinking, it could have been Wales. I think we would have done quite well there, if we'd adjusted to the heat.'

It's more than 35 years since Wales last got to the World Cup finals – that was in Sweden in 1958 – but when they did they made it through the first round after winning a play-off against Hungary 2–1. They lost in the next round to Brazil when a little known striker called Pele scored a lucky deflection that proved decisive. France 1998 could see Giggs against Romario and a chance for revenge on those Brazilians.

Control and Passing

We've talked about lots of skills so far, but in football you must never neglect the basics – control and accurate passing. They're so important. It's Ryan Giggs' ability to control the ball that makes him better than his Premier League rivals. He looks better because he has made more time on the ball.

Ryan Giggs

'All the players I most admire seem to have time on the ball. It's because they control it well. They make time. The first thing my coaches taught me was to control the ball. It meant I could look up before passing. I had more time to find a pal. And he, in turn, had more time to score.

You can control the ball with any part of your body – except your hands! There's the top of your foot, or your chest; your thigh can take the sting out of it. The end result should be the ball at your feet.

Once you've 'killed it' you can start thinking about using it. Then you've got to weigh up which of your team mates is best placed to exploit possession. Some of them may be out of reach. If that's the case, then leave them out of it. The worst thing you can

Be a cushion

The great players all have terrific control of the ball. It always seems to drop at their feet, no matter how hard the pass to them was. The ball is moving fast, then it's dead. They take the pace out of it. When you've got to control the ball with your thigh or your chest, you have to cushion the ball, otherwise it will end up away from your feet. You must be relaxed and be prepared to move so that you can meet the ball using the part of your body that's easiest for you to take the sting out of the ball with. And, like Ryan here, you've got to watch it on to your thigh so you know when to cushion its fall.

do with possession after showing good control is to give it away.

You can pass to a pal with any part of your foot, just as long as it gets there! You can use your instep to side foot it – that's very accurate – or, if you need more power, use the laced part of your boot. By altering your approach to the ball you can put swerve on it to bend it around defenders to team mates in space. The Brazilians are fantastic at that. They use the outsides of their feet as well. You can too, if you practise. And, in case you've forgotten, watch the ball and follow through. It should go without saying now.'

Practising your control and passing (left) may not be the most exciting part of improving your soccer skills, but you may as well give up any hope of being a good player if you're not prepared to spend the time doing it and getting the basics right. It means a lot of time with a pal or against a wall, just passing and controlling, but it will be worth it.

Bobby Charlton
'Ryan's lucky. His control is good. It saves him time. The sooner you learn control the better. The Brazilians are always practising controlling the ball quickly, taking the sting out of it so they can do something creative with it. They're always ready for the ball, always on their toes, always moving to make control easier. That's what you've got to be like. Ready to control the ball to give you more time to make that killer pass.

Your body's like a cushion. When the ball drops on a cushion it dies. That's what your control should be like so the ball drops just in front of your toes. Dead. Further away and the defender's going to get it. If it comes to your wrong foot – for Ryan, that's his right – then use it. You'll save time.

It's difficult to control with your wrong foot. But good control – and the good techniques for passing that Ryan's mentioned – comes with practice. Against a wall on your own, or with a pal in the park, it's the only way. Don't be one of those footballers who neglects the basics. Even when you're the best in your team there will be other players you haven't met who will be better.'

Finishing

It's in the net. Get in there. A goal. Brilliant! It's the whole reason why we practise the skills in this book; to improve the chances of us scoring a goal. Ryan Giggs is no different. He wants more skills to score more goals. This last discipline, finishing, is to make sure your hard work on other attacking skills is rewarded with exactly that. Then you can start to think about celebrating.

It's there. The striker has seen a chance and made the effort to get on the end of it for a goal. The tackle went in from behind, but even though the rules have been amended after the World Cup, it's not a foul. He's played the ball. That's fine. It's a brave effort. The striker could have got injured, but if you go in to a challenge determined to get the ball, you will probably not get hurt. Here, it needed just a touch in front of the defender who is almost on the line and it's in.

Ryan Giggs

'Everybody loves goals. The fans want them, I want them. If I don't score, I can't celebrate. They don't have to be 20-yarders. A tap-in can give as much pleasure. It can simply be the occasion that makes a goal special.

At the finish to our second Premiership-winning season, when people started to say we were going to blow it like we did in 1992, we played one of our last games at Ipswich. We went 1–0 down and the talk was that we'd got the jitters again. It wasn't looking good.

Eric Cantona scored and got us back into the game and we began to play quite well, although I wasn't getting into any scoring positions. Then Roy Keane got free on the right and crossed it into the box. Luckily I got on the end of it. I was pretty chuffed about it, even though I was only about a yard out. (I wasn't so chuffed about being substituted later!) But we won, and clinched the title again. My goal against Ipswich proved crucial. It wasn't a great goal by any means, but afterwards I felt fantastic. Just putting the ball in the net was enough.

A few seasons ago, I counted up about ten chances that I'd missed when I should have scored. They were straightforward finishes and it irritated me. I decided to be more determined in front of goal after that. I've always played as a striker or as an attacking midfielder, but finishing has been a weakness in my game. I'd get into great scoring positions all right, but the number of goals at the end of the season was sometimes disappointing.

I realized I was there or thereabouts when the chances came, but I was just standing around and watching. I just thought, I've got to get in there, get among defenders, get on the end of crosses and through balls. It doesn't matter how you score. Finishing is all about making the best out of a situation. We've covered all the skills you'll need to score. All that's left is for you to be determined enough to make them pay.

You can always make sure that you're alert and on your toes. When the chance comes, you must be ready. If you're ready to receive the ball, you'll be ready to stick it in the net.

The goal against Ipswich wasn't a great goal. I just about got my toe on it. But all the great finishers – Gary Lineker, one of my heroes, Ian Rush – all score from two yards out as well as 20 yards. They're always ready. You must be, too. It's the best way to make the most out of the skills you've learnt and the hard work you've put in.'

Bobby Charlton

'I remember that goal against Ipswich. I was out of my seat. United had won the title again. Brilliant.

Ryan was like a two-year-old after he scored. I've never seen him celebrate so much. He was jumping up and down and punching the air.

That's what scoring does to you. It makes you happy! Ryan's not the most expressive of players, even after a goal, but it was a great moment for him.

Everyone who loves football wants to enjoy the

same sort of moment. I'm sure you do. But we can't all score the winner for Manchester United. But even when you know you're not going to be as good as someone like Ryan Giggs, there's still the time that you're playing for your team with your pals and you do something brilliant like scoring. Then it's great because all your hard work on skills has paid off.

Being ready is the key to finishing, as Ryan says. Nobody scores many goals waiting for the ball. Attack it, particularly in the penalty box.

You can unsettle defenders, too, while you're waiting for a cross. It will help make the finish easier as it will give you more time. All the great players

The danger zone – the penalty box and six-yard area – is where matches are won and lost. When you find yourself in there, you've got to be prepared to go for the ball and really take advantage of the opportunity your team mates' good possession has created. Here, for Manchester United against Oldham, there are two attackers – Roy Keane and Giggs – on the ball which is a good sign. They both got in behind the defence and, on this occasion the ball ended up in the net. It was worth the effort in the end, particularly for Giggs who was credited with the goal. Then you're free to acknowledge the cheers and have a celebratory jig.

can unsettle defenders without the ball. Bob and weave, do a few dummy runs and decoy moves. They will all go to helping you score when the chance finally comes your way.

The other crucial thing with finishing is confidence. Be confident. With the skills you've learnt, you'll have the ability to beat defenders and the keeper. Don't be afraid to bend it, chip it, place it, and whatever you chose to do, HAVE A GO if you get a chance.

I'm not saying that everyone can be as confident or as good as Ryan Giggs. They can't. But everyone can be better at their game. And everyone wants to score. So work hard and don't be afraid to miss. I was really lucky to be a footballer. I got paid to do something I'd have done for nothing. It wasn't really work, for me it was just a pleasure to play. You may not be good enough to be a professional, like Ryan, but it is still worth practising in the park or playground for the moment when you are faced with a situation requiring some skill.

Good finishing is no different to any other skill we've tried to help you with in this book. In fact, it's as important as any because good finishing means goals. And goals are what it is all about. Whether it's at Old Trafford or in your back garden.'

The Future

Ryan Giggs has it all to come. He's already won a clean sweep of domestic honours, but the best moments of his career lie ahead of him. It's an exciting thought for his fans and for followers of Wales and Manchester United. Ryan's already thrilled them with many of the skills you've read about in this book. And there's surely more in store!

'Sometimes I have to pinch myself about it all. When I started playing, my team mates were my heroes. The important thing has been not to be overawed by it all. My mates have been brilliant. (They still are!) Most of them are Manchester United fans and come to watch the games. If I've had a bad game they'll always remind me how lucky I am. They are mainly from school and the best thing is they haven't changed at all since I made the first team.'

On the pitch, his ambitions with United focus on the European Cup: 'It's a long time since United won it in 1968. It would be great to do it. A lot of comparisons have been made between the present team and that one. Hopefully we can achieve what they did.'

Off the pitch, there's the promotional work, commitments to various charities which Ryan takes very seriously, and the chance to meet new people and visit new places on holiday or with Manchester United and Wales.

'I've been to Antigua and the club's trip to South Africa in 1993 was really enjoyable. I had no idea how big United were there. None of the team realized how many fans we had. We were introduced to Nelson Mandela, too. It was a great thrill meeting him.

'Promotional work can be quite fun. I really enjoyed making the television programme and video that go with this book. It's good to know that people reading and watching want to be the next Eric Cantona, the next Mark Hughes, or even the next Ryan Giggs, and want to play for Manchester United like I always did.'

The attention of the Media has to be dealt with too. Ryan is becoming more and more confident in this area where the greatest asset is experience. 'The manager has a policy of keeping young players away from the Press so that they can concentrate on their football without worrying about a lot of interviews. We had some training on dealing with the Media when we were apprentices – how to answer questions and look into the camera – which has helped with the pressures that off-field attention can bring.'

But, for the foreseeable future, the football will always come first. It's Ryan's priority. 'The main thing is football. As I've said, I am lucky to be doing what I'm doing. And when people talk about what I've done to date and say that I've made it, I always remember that I have a lot to improve on.'

'Obviously, at a club like Manchester United, you've always got to set yourself the target of staying in the first team. The competition for places is very intense. The squad is full of internationals in every position, including mine. First team football is my priority.'

Like you, Ryan still wants to improve his skills. His schedule for the future includes plenty of time to refine the abilities that have helped him accomplish what he already has in the game and will help him achieve his future goals.

'I can still learn a lot from players like Eric Cantona, from the way he practises, his dedication and his overall range. I've got some targets that I've set myself which I hope I can meet. I take each day as it comes. Ten years ago, I wouldn't have dreamed I'd be playing for Manchester United. You just never know how things are going to work out.'

They only thing for sure is there will be plenty of practise on soccer skills. It's what got Ryan Giggs to where he is today with United and with Wales.

Ryan has already achieved in football what many players would be satisfied with over a whole career. He's pretty popular with the fans, too and that means signing quite a lot of autographs! But Ryan knows he's lucky to be playing football.